Also by the same author:

ROYAL VISIT TO TONGA (Pitkin, 1954)

THE FRIENDLY ISLANDERS (Hodder and Stoughton, 1967)

A GUIDE TO PITCAIRN (Ed.) (British South Pacific Office, 1970)

TREASON AT TEN: Fiji at the Crossroads (Hodder and Stoughton, 1989)

THE NEW FRIENDLY ISLANDERS (Hodder and Stoughton, 1993)

St Helena

The Island,
Her People and Their Ship

KENNETH BAIN

First published in Great Britain in 1993

by

WILTON 65
Flat Top House, Bishop Wilton, York.

ISBN 0 947828 17 6

Printed & Bound
by
Garden House Press Ltd.

For Margaret, an island girl of the South Pacific.

CONTENTS

Foreword by HRH Prince Andrew, Duke of York

Chapter		Page
1	Islands	1
2	Saints	6
3	Voyage 6 South: Self-examination	14
4	Officers & Passengers	24
5	When the Saints ...	30
6	The Landing	34
7	New Year's Day	38
8	Fallibility	43
9	Change	46
10	The Governor	51
11	Justice	58
12	Eric	62
13	The City	67
14	Notices	72
15	The Fax of Life	79
16	Bridge Passage: Captain Bligh & the Breadfruit	84
17	Past Poetic Licence at Plantation	91
18	Island of Exiles	95
19	Father Christmas	100
20	The Has and the Has-nots	107
21	*Oman Sea One*	112
22	A Swain of Tristan	120
23	Tristan da Cunha: An Island on Its Own Terms	122
24	A South Pacific Tristan da Cunha	142
25	Voyage 6 North: Re-examination	149
26	Birth of a Ship	156
27	The Contract	172
28	'Let Go Fore and Aft'	178
	Appendix I - History	179
	Appendix II - Governors	185
	Appendix III - From *The Times* 2nd December 1840	187
	Acknowledgements	189
	Editor's Note	191
	Index	192

WATERMARK DRAWINGS
OF
ENDEMIC PLANTS

	Page
Bastard Gumwood (Commidendrum rotundifolium)	13
Tree Fern (Dicksonia arborescens)	13
Small Bellflower (Wahlenbergia angustifolia)	23
Polypodium Dianæ	33
St. Helena Rosemary (Phylica polifolia)	42
Large Bellflower (Wahlenbergia linfolia)	45
Old Father Live Forever (Pelargonium cotyledonia)	45
Black Cabbage Tree (Melanodendron integrifolium)	57
Baby's Toes (Hydrodea cryptantha)	106
St. Helena Plantain (Plantago robusta)	106
She Cabbage Tree (Lachanodes arborea)	171
False Gumwood (Commidendrum spurium)	171
Dogwood (Nesohedyotis arborea)	177
Scrubwood (Commidendrum rugosum)	177
He Cabbage Tree (detail) Pladaroxylon leucadendron	184
Redwood (Trochetiopsis erythroxylon)	184

ILLUSTRATIONS

LINE DRAWINGS

Sketch map of St.Helena	Frontispiece
	Page
Outline sketch map of South Atlantic	5
St. Martin-in-the-Hills	12
RMS St. Helena at anchor	29
Cage landing passengers at Jamestown	36
The Briars Pavilion	66
Count Bertrand's House	66
French tricolour flag	66
Skipjack Tuna and Barracuda	71
St. Helena Aloe (Furcraea gigantia)	76
South Atlantic Post Office Memorial stone - 1645	78
First Day Cover - 13th September 1990	83
Breadfruit tree, with details of fruit and foliage	90
Visitor's book, Plantation House	94
Boer Cemetery at Knoolcombes	98
Wirebird	110
Cable & Wireless Facsimile and Telephone Directory	111
Immigration Visa stamp - Tristan da Cunha	125
Albatross off Tristan da Cunha	141
Sketch map of Tristan da Cunha	148
Crayfish	155
Flower of Black Cabbage Tree (Melanodendron Integrifolium)	186
Whitewood Cabbage Tree (Petrobium Arboreum)	186

COLOURED ILLUSTRATIONS
Between pages 78 & 79

PLATE No.

I   *RMS St. Helena* works her cargo at anchor off Jamestown

II   Downtown Jamestown from half way up Jacob's Ladder

III   Under the shade away from the mid-day sun

IV   Jacob's Ladder rises 602ft from Jamestown to the top of Ladder Hill. 699 steps. A long way up, or down.

V   Plantation House. The Governor's residence since 1792

VI   Delia, Mrs. Alan Hoole, wife of the Governor, seated in the hall at Plantation House 1992

VII   The Post Office from where mail is both posted and collected

VIII Flagstaff and The Barn

IX   Lush vegetation in the highlands gives way to barren landscape at sea level

X   Gateway to the Castle. Seat of the Government of St.Helena

XI   Success! Fishing with rod and line is a pastime most Saints enjoy

COLOURED ILLUSTRATIONS
Between Pages 120 & 121

PLATE No.

XII   Ceremony abounds when the Chief Justice comes to open a Session of the Supreme Court

XIII   Longwood House, home of the exiled Emperor Napoleon Bonaparte

XIV   High Knoll Fort, built originally by British troops stationed on the Island to protect it from attack by the French. It now serves as the Animal Quarantine Station

XV   Sandy Bay Baptist Chapel serves the small community in the south of the Island

XVI   School Sports Day is always on New Years Day - every one is there to cheer on their team

XVII   Smiling faces on Sports Day

XVIII   The Island's only Gaol is home to its occasional inmates

XIX   John Musk's General Store stocks groceries exported to St. Helena from Great Britain and South Africa

XX   The Potato Patches. Potatoes were once the currency of the Island of Tristan da Cunha

XXI   Tristan's houses are built of local stone

XXII   Seals off Tristan da Cunha are normally not disturbed by tourists

XXIII   Sailing long boats are the pride and joy of Tristan men. It is important to tie them down to avoid damage by wind

FOREWORD BY HRH PRINCE ANDREW
DUKE OF YORK

BUCKINGHAM PALACE

It has been ten years since I visited St. Helena. I recall vividly my arrival and the warmth of the welcome I received. I was sadly only in the island for a few days but in that short time I was able to experience a life full of diversity and history.

The island relies on a lifeline provided by R.M.S. St. Helena which I launched in Aberdeen in 1989. I revisited the ship in Cardiff Docks just before Christmas and on the eve of the voyage south. I had the privilege of sharing with the officers and crew at first hand - both British and Saints - the great pride they all have in serving the island community.

This book tells a story about an island that is isolated in the South Atlantic, visited infrequently because of its geographic position, but full of history, social diversity and family values.

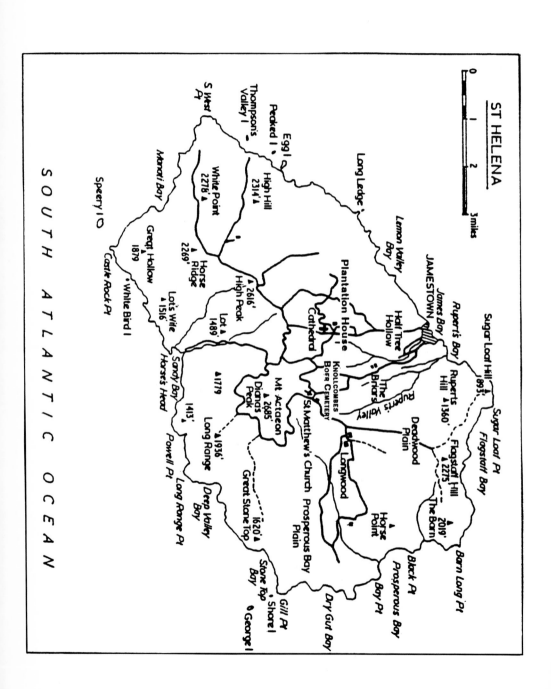

CHAPTER 1

Islands

There are islands and islands. Some are tiny, like a thousand reef-girt pin points in the South Pacific. One - Australia - is vast, the distance between Perth in the west and Sydney in the east being almost that between London and Moscow. Some burst with vitality, their skylines constantly changing, like Hong Kong and Singapore. Some smoke and rumble, like White Island off mainland New Zealand. Some are offshoots of huge land masses, like Vancouver, Tasmania and Newfoundland. Some are flat coralline and vulnerable, like those of The Maldives. So too Micronesian Kiribati, with islands connected by causeways - open when the tide is low, submerged when it is high. Its thirty-six islands have a total land area of 281 square miles, spread over an astonishing two million square miles of ocean. Some islands are volcanic and mountainous, like Tenerife whose El Teide rises to a height of 12,195 feet, the highest point in the North and South Atlantic and matching that of Mt. Cook in the Southern Alps of New Zealand.

Some are close and accessible and may thus go unnoticed, like the Isle of Wight. Some have apparently silly names like Turks and Caicos and, well, the Scillies. Some are remote and inaccessible, like Tristan da Cunha and Pitcairn, and have thus been islands of refuge. Some have been penitentiaries, like Robben Island in the bay of Cape Town, Alcatraz and Devil's Island. Some were places of exile, like Elba and St. Helena. Some were fortresses of wartime fortitude, like Malta. Some are divided, like Cyprus and strife-torn Sri Lanka. Some have erupted, like Tristan da Cunha and Niuafo'ou in Tonga. One or two even disappear beneath the ocean from time to time, like Falcon, otherwise Jack-in-the-box island, also in Tonga. Some have warm and friendly climates, their women relaxed and available in the perceptions of visiting sailors, like the islands of French Polynesia.

Some live in snowbound isolation and darkness for much of the northern winter, like Greenland which fails to live up to its name and Iceland which doesn't either. Some are earthy, brash and brassy, like the reggae music of their Caribbean. Some are of divine beauty, like the British Virgin Islands and the Seychelles. Some are culturally vibrant but with shattering poverty, like Jamaica and Puerto Rico. Some are multi-racial and live within sight of social and economic success, like Mauritius. Some have already achieved it, like Singapore while repressing the voice of opposition. Or had it, like Fiji, until it was jettisoned as a consequence of the military destruction of a democratically elected government in 1987.

Then there are fictional islands of romance and legendary treasure and Desert Island Disc escapism, like those of Daniel Defoe and Robert Louis Stevenson. There are shared islands like Hispaniola, with the coup-prone and voodoo-ridden poverty of French-speaking Haiti placed uneasily beside the cock-fight pits of the Spanish-speaking Dominican Republic. Only the ocean binds their lands together. Some are islands of mystery like Easter, with its great ancient Polynesian stone statues. And there is the island of a thousand tongues - Papua New Guinea - where the stone age rubs shoulders with that of computers.

Some ... but the list of comparisons and differences is endless; not least within the great archipelagic countries like Indonesia with a population of 180 million and 13,677 islands, 6,000 inhabited; and between the rich and the poor, like the equatorial Republic of Nauru, twelve miles round, rich in the proceeds of phosphate workings and, at one time, second only to Kuwait in *per capita* wealth. Compare this with the frugal lives of the Polynesian, Micronesian and Melanesian atoll dwellers of the South Pacific or of those who seek to survive in the cardboard tenements of the less favoured islands of the Caribbean.

I come from an island country and the Scottish city of Dunedin in the South Island of New Zealand. I grew up with a child's awareness of the pounding power of the breakers of an ill-tempered Pacific

Ocean on cold beaches. It confined and separated us from the cultural riches of the older worlds of Europe, Asia and the Americas. Thus insularity and its bed-fellow isolationism can be bred, and strange parochial things done to balanced perspectives in an intrusive world. On tiny Pitcairn Island in the mid-1960s, an Australian-born woman was the postmistress. She was married to a Pitcairner and had lived on the island for more than twenty-five years, the only 'foreigner' to do so then. Yet, after a quarter of a century, she was still described as 'The Stranger.' No one used her real name when she was mentioned in conversation.

Those who live within land borders and police posts with national dividing lines often drawn capriciously across desert or forest, cannot easily comprehend how it can be to live among a handful of people totally surrounded by limitless unbroken sea. Calm and tempest follow each other as day does night. Hazard and succour are together and at one in an all-embracing ocean. Side by side with the simple concept of sharing, the essence of 'cargo cult' cupidity may be latent in every small islander. And small island community life contains - or restrains - ambition by welcoming the concept and resisting its realisation.

Until its move to Bedford Square in December 1992, the Royal Institute of Public Administration, and its successor RIPA International Ltd., was a salubrious sanctuary in one of central London's great royal parks. It is sublime in spring or autumn, not least for those from tropical climates who experience the northern seasons for the first time. In October 1991 Ivy Ellick, Chief Personnel Officer of the Government of St. Helena, was attending a RIPA course in Management and National Development. She had journeyed by sea to London with her husband Ray, the Chief Development Officer for St. Helena. He was to undergo complex back surgery in London.

The most experienced member of the course was Daphne de Rebello, joint Secretary at the Ministry of Education in New Delhi.

"I just cannot imagine," Daphne said to Ivy one day, "I just cannot conceive of living where you do, what that is like. How can it be? A whole island country and people - the size of an Indian village - miles from anywhere in isolated mid-ocean."

Ivy smiled. She was used to this. "We manage. We Saints are pretty resourceful - all things considered - in our small South Atlantic home."

Daphne was not persuaded. "So you say, but I still don't see ... one ship in four weeks and no airport. It doesn't make sense to me."

An understandable reaction, I thought, if you are nurtured in a semi-ungovernable country of nine hundred million, ethnically and linguistically fragmented; a country which clings precariously to the principles and some at least of the practices of democracy.

"You should try it and see," Ivy said indulgently. "Then it might come to make sense to you."

Try it and see. Yes, I thought. Why not? For a third time of asking. That is what I should do. Before it is too late. Try St. Helena again - and see.

* * *

I went to the Commonwealth Institute at the beginning of November 1991. The Institute, in the fashionable Kensington of West London, is an ever-changing visual kaleidoscope of Commonwealth riches - historical, human, cultural, social and economic. It never fails to impress its visitors from within Britain and beyond. But it disappointed me that day.

I approached an aging, seemingly preoccupied Asian attendant, clad in grey slacks and natty logo-identifying blazer. "Do you have a corner for St. Helena?"

He looked puzzled. His eyes wandered. "What, sir, is that? Is that a Commonwealth country you are speaking of? Not some religious lady?"

"Well, it is by association. But it is not an independent state. It is a British dependent territory. In the South Atlantic."

He looked relieved, confidence restored. "No, sir. Not that one. We only have Commonwealth countries here, you see. No, no. Not that one."

He shuffled off. Definitely. So did I and stopped beneath a great Chinese lion head. 'A gift from Hong Kong' the notice said. I wondered how he would explain that being there - for a few more years anyway ... Recognition of the irony was to come later - in St. Helena itself.

CHAPTER 2

Saints

Is it possible to write about St. Helena and not about Napoleon Bonaparte, his exile there in 1815, his terminal agonies, his death in 1821 and his repatriation to reburial below the south dome of Les Invalides in Paris? I am going to try, not least because enough has already been written. Indeed, more ink has probably been spent analysing, dissecting, interpreting and pronouncing on that imperatorial life than any other such. There can be nothing new to say, not least in respect of those painful last years of exile at The Briars and Longwood House on St. Helena.

Yet I won't be entirely successful: the long Napoleonic shadow lives on into the present with the maintenance by the French Government of the residence and of the near-sacred earth upon which the Emperor walked in his last years. Presiding over all this has been a possessive and, some say, eccentric semi-resident French consul. Now responsibility has passed to his son.

The French tricoleur flies, not over ceded French territory as has been supposed; but, as Governor Alan Hoole revealed to me, freehold owned by the French Government. We were standing, not inappropriately, beneath the chandelier at Plantation House which used to be above Napoleon's dining table at Longwood. It was about to be returned there.

Revive more frequent passenger shipping to St. Helena, put up a few modest hostelries, and the narrow streets of Jamestown and beyond will be stretched to cope with mass migrations up the hill to the imperial shrine. If St. Helena were in the Caribbean, Napoleon would be declared an honorary citizen on the two hundredth anniversary in 2015 of his enforced arrival. Imported Napoleon brandy would be blended and bottled in St. Helena and marketed throughout the world by short squat men in black tricornes, frock coats with epaulettes, shimmering pantaloons and knee-high black boots. A sort of companion for Pussers Rum from the British Virgin Islands.

Sir Robert Ricketts is an avid historian and authority on the years of Napoleon's exile on St. Helena. His wife, Theresa, is the younger daughter of Sir Stafford Cripps who was Chancellor of the Exchequer in Clement Attlee's 1945-1951 Labour Government. The Ricketts were travelling to St. Helena for their first visit. Two days out of Jamestown, he gave a thoughtful and precisely delivered lecture of forty minutes entitled 'Napoleon - The St. Helena Years.'

When it was over it was Lady Ricketts who told me that her husband had not written publicly about Napoleon. "There have been quite enough, I think."

"How many?" I asked, naïvety and ignorance revealed at the same time.

"About 250 in French and English on the last years in exile. But many more on Napoleon's life as a whole. There was a real industry."

"How many?" I asked again.

"The figure I have been given is some 8,000 - 10,000 volumes and pamphlets, not including articles."

Thank God, I said to myself, that I had not thought of attempting what might have been number 10,001.

"What," I asked Sir Robert Ricketts, much later en route to Tristan, "surprised you most when you first saw and entered Longwood?"

"I suppose," he said, reflecting, "I suppose how small the dining room is with its big table. The staff must have had great difficulty in serving when all the entourage were present for dinner."

"The bath?"

"Yes, the depth of the bath. Napoleon used to recline in it for long periods, with hot water constantly being poured in, to try to relieve the pain in his stomach."

In spite of its remoteness in the South Atlantic, there is a surprising number of visitors to Longwood House. I had added up the signatures for 1991 in the visitors' book. There were 1,100. If one in four or five were to bother to sign, perhaps 5,000 people had made the expensive pilgrimage in one year to kindle a sense of the last years of Napoleon Bonaparte.

So we must look back just a little - even earlier in fact - to achieve a sense of perspective for today and tomorrow in St. Helena.

The date to put in your diary is 21st May, 2002. On that day, five hundred years before, the Portuguese navigator Bartholomew Diaz sighted a high peak in the South Atlantic ocean. Admiral Juan da Nova Castella was bringing three ships to reinforce the Portuguese base and trading posts in Calicut, West India.

"When at last he rounded the tempestuous Cape of Good Hope" says Philip Gosse in the 1990 edition of 'St. Helena 1502 - 1938', "da Nova ran his ships before the steady south-east trade wind; and it was on 21st May 1502, the anniversary of St. Helena, mother of the Emperor Constantine, that the sailor at the masthead cried 'land ho' and on the horizon could be made out a lofty island. In honour of the Saint, da Nova at once christened the unknown island and new possession of the King of Portugal, Saint Helena."

Somewhat later, in 1975 to be precise, another astute man of the sea, Andrew Bell, founded a small company called Curnow Shipping in the tiny Cornish fishing port of Porthleven. "Curnow is the anglicised version of Kerno" said Bell, in response to my question, "and Kerno is Cornish for Cornwall."

If you had not heard before of Curnow Shipping, your life will not have been in vain. Andrew Bell would not be surprised. Some 5,500 Saints though, might find that unbelievable. We shall see why.

Saints? The self-styled people of St. Helena, that is, who inhabit the lonely, supposedly neglected, South Atlantic outpost of British colonial remnant territory. I have never understood how it is, constitutionally, that one dependent territory can in turn spawn two others. Nonetheless, the Colony of St. Helena has duly done so: Ascension Island to the north and Tristan da Cunha to the south. Each has an Administrator responsible to the Governor of St. Helena who resides in eighteenth century graciousness at Plantation House, above Jamestown.

Neglected, it could be argued with some justification in respect of St. Helena a decade or so ago. Not anymore, is it ignored or forgotten.

A certain ship, the *RMS St. Helena* - with those who fund it and those who operate it - is indisputable evidence of this. As too is the still new Prince Andrew School and its assembly and community hall. In 1991, annual financial support from London to the government and people of St. Helena was running at about £8,000,000 for the shipping subsidy, budgetary aid, technical assistance and funding for various capital projects. A figure of about £1,500 for every adult and child on St. Helena must be the highest annual recurrent contribution ever made to a British dependent territory. It is equivalent to 75% of what an unskilled St. Helena workman earns at home in a year.

And it is because of the ship that the last island of Napoleon Bonaparte has been burdened, some contend, by a succession of ocean-travelling, time-consuming and boringly disagreeing so-called experts from Britain who have descended with awesome frequency - whether its people wanted them or not - to propound this or that theory for economic or social or agricultural development. Then, having done so they would, like me, leave on the next voyage or the one thereafter to be, for evermore, the embodiment of instant wisdom about South Atlantic island life. Except, that is, on St. Helena itself.

Sometimes it is the other way. Tommy George had been to London for the first time, to represent the Legislative Council of St. Helena at the thirty second annual assembly of the Commonwealth Parliamentary Association. I flew with him from RAF Station Brize Norton to Ascension Island in 1986; thence via the old RMS to St. Helena.

Tommy was welcomed back in grand island style. After all, he had made it to the big time for St. Helena - and Tommy. There was a Council lunch in his honour.

"Come on Tommy. Tell us about it. What was it really like? We wait too long."

"Well" said Tommy "I tell you. Some werry strange t'ings happen in that big conference place in London where we all gather. The 'security' they call it. Every toime I go in an' I go out, they put a machine all over my legs an' chest an' other places, buzz buzz buzz jus' loike flies roun' a chicken arse. Then they ask me to speak 'bout St. Helena so I say all right I do that. But when the toime come, do you know what happen?"

"No Tommy, we don' know. Tell us Tommy, tell us. That what we waitin' to hear. That what we sen' you for in the firs' place. Tell us."

"Well I was goin' to, but you talk too much. O.K. This what happen. Here I am speakin' all 'bout St. Helena an' people are gettin' up an' going out an' comin' in and out talkin' to each other. I tell you. They not polite there in London. In that Parliament meetin'. They don' pay attenshun. We far more sophisticate in our Council in St. Helena. Don' you agree Ken?"

The spotlight; an appeal for help and instant corroboration. Couldn't I look away, uninvolved, stay silent? Not my affair really. Have another sandwich?

"Don' you agree Ken? Ken, you hearin' me?"

No avoiding it. Here goes. "Well, yes, Tommy is right I guess. They do those things, politicians that is, in London. Go in and out of the House of Commons, not listening. All very discourteous at times, it would seem. Nothing like that is done in the Legislative Council of St. Helena, I have no doubt."

"There you are" said Tommy, beaming with delight. "Ken know a t'ing or two. He been aroun'. Prove my point. We far more sophisticate in our Council in St. Helena that those politishun in London."

The Second Mate on Voyage 6 South and North was Rodney Young. He is a Saint - in the St. Helenian sense. He does not like to be described as Second Officer because it reminds him of Union Castle. Hardly anyone calls him Rodney, let alone Mr. Young. He is School Bus, a nickname apparently bestowed in his early years and which has stuck. The reasons are apparent when you see and hear him. He is shortish, plump, squat and forthright. An action man. And there are times when the Little Napoleon that is behind the genial face of School Bus bursts out.

I witnessed an example when I came on board the *RMS* at Cardiff to place my baggage in the cabin. I needed a second journey down the gangway to my car.

"Where are you going?" asked a shoreside security man.

"To get the rest of my baggage."

"No one can go ashore until all the passengers have embarked. Those are my orders."

"I am not a visitor. I am a passenger."

"Then please show me your embarkation card."

"I don't have one. I am getting on in Tenerife and putting my baggage on here."

"Then you are not a passenger and yours is unaccompanied baggage. That is loaded after the passengers' baggage and when it has been cleared by Customs. You cannot go ashore until all the passengers are on board."

It was only an hour before sailing and still raining heavily.

"But look ..."

"I'm sorry. Those are my instructions."

"But look indeed," said an anonymous figure at the head of the gangway. He was wearing a tin hat and heavy blue coat. He was very wet. I did not know that he was the Second Mate. "But look indeed," he said again in a voice of penetrating authority. "I don't know what your instructions are intended to achieve; but mine are to get this ship ready for sailing at 4 p.m. sharp. That is the absolute limit through the locks if we are to catch the tide. If we miss, we are held here until tomorrow. We cannot be delayed - by anything. Do you understand **that**?" He glowered at the wilting security man.

"Well, yes, all right. In the circumstances. Provided he is accompanied by a senior member of the ship's staff."

"Come with me" said the Chief Purser and put on a blue raincoat.

"I know a back way."

Napoleon faded from the face of School Bus and Saintly sunshine returned through the rain.

"Well, that's fixed then," he said and turned to the next problem.

Weeks later he was on the bridge in neat white shirt, shorts, long socks and shoes. When he is at home, he lives in Upper Jamestown.

"If you walk down past the houses on Sunday morning," he said, "all you hear is the BBC Sunday service, from one radio after another. Every third Sunday or so it comes from St. Martin in the Fields. So every Saint knows that church. Or think they do. When we get back to Cardiff, we usually have so little time off that all the crew can do is go into the city, do their shopping and come back. Hardly ever to London. But on one voyage arrangements were made for eight stewards, greasers and deckhands to go to Gravesend for a week's fire course. Although they had all been with the company for about twelve years, none of them had been to London before. All they wanted to do was two things - to visit Madame Tussaud's and the Church of St. Martin in the Fields."

St.MARTIN-in-the-HILLS

"So on the Saturday, they set out and found their way by themselves to Madame Tussaud's at Baker Street underground station. Then they got on the bus to take them to the church. When the bus reached Trafalgar Square, the conductor said 'This is where you get off. That's St. Martin in the Fields over there.' And they said, 'No, it isn't. It can't be.' And they refused to get off the bus. The conductor said, 'Well you can please yourself. That's it all right.' Finally they got off and stood outside on the pavement. Bewildered and disappointed they could not believe what they saw in Trafalgar Square. All they could say was 'You go up to our little St. Martin in the Hills in St. Helena an' you see some fine hills roun' t'at. T'at why it call t'at.'

School Bus was getting excited. "They said 'How you 'spec' us to b'lieve t'at is St. Martin in the Fields when all t'ose building roun' it an' no fields?'"

He shook with laughter as he turned back to the electronic screens and technological marvels on the bridge of the *RMS*. "Whoops" he said as a great bow wave burst over the foredeck and smacked against the broad windows and windscreen wipers of the bridge. "You better duck."

CHAPTER 3

Voyage 6 South: Self-Examination

The *RMS* duly sailed out through the locks of Cardiff to the Bristol Channel, Land's End and south to Tenerife on Tuesday, 17th December, 1991. It did so in streaming rain and in the teeth of a force 8 gale, my heavy baggage safely on board. I drove four hundred miles that day in fog, rain, gales and M25 and M4 motorway jams, from Sevenoaks in Kent to Cardiff in Wales, and back. It was exhausting but somehow preferable to pitching into that force 8 south-westerly in the Channel.

I flew from Gatwick to Tenerife on Friday, 20th December. There the temperature was 70°, the sky a benign blue and the sea white-flaked and active. I was booked into the Hotel Atlantico in Santa Cruz by the Curnow Agents. It was a friendly two-star hotel with a flair for informal hospitality from young staff. Marble and mirrors abounded. There were two nights to wait before the *RMS* came in. The shaded darkness of the bedroom overlooking a Spanish inner courtyard was a relief from the brilliance of a sun I had again to get used to. "So you are doing the chicken run," Clive Warren had said when I told him what I proposed to do. I had called at the new offices of the Overseas Development Administration (the British Government's overseas aid agency in London's Victoria Street).

"The chicken run? What's that?"

"Those who chicken out of the Bay of Biscay going south," he laughed. "Not that I blame you, I did it myself once." Clive Warren was the desk officer for St. Helena from 1984 to 1989. In my view, his sustained energy was largely responsible for a peak time in the developmental fortunes of St. Helena.

I slept or rested for most of what remained of Friday; walked in the evening and slept again. On Saturday I went to lunch with Victor Gonzales Dust. At 70, he was the owner and head of Southern Agencies, a small company with a staff of six, the agents for Curnow

Shipping in the Canary Islands. His office is on the fifth floor of Hamilton House overlooking the modest man-made harbour of Santa Cruz de Tenerife.

Victor Dust was born in London of an English mother and a Spanish father. When he was only a few months old, the family moved to Paris where they stayed for twenty years. He was there during the German occupation of France and taught himself German for the purpose. He is a master of five languages, the others being French, Spanish, Italian and English. His spoken English is syntactically precise and polished. He paints, mainly water colours. Musically, his interests fall short of Bach and Wagner, but range from Vivaldi and Haydn to Lutoslawski and Dutilleux. Plus the New Orleans jazz of Jelly Roll Morton and Kid Ory. He married into the Spanish landed aristocracy; and is still slightly bewildered by how it happened and by the disciplines imposed domestically upon him as a consequence.

"In which language do you prefer to write?" I asked.

"Oh English, without a doubt. And I am not being polite to you or disrespectful to my other languages. It is just that the richness of the imagery and the vocabulary is not matched by any of them. And then there is the question of fantasy. Do you know that Spanish children have no fairy stories? Fantasy is regarded as lies and as such is condemned by the Church. Spanish children are treated and are thus expected to behave as 'little adults' from the beginning of their lives."

Victor Dust was French Consul in Tenerife for two long periods until Mitterand became President. "I hate Socialists and Socialism. You can't serve a government whose policies you despise. So I resigned. Anyhow, I don't care much for transplanted democracy or the interpretation of democracy I have experienced. It leads to feeble government. And I am not sure that is good for anyone. A degree of authoritarianism is necessary for a nation as well as a family." On that premise the Saints were luckier than they may appreciate to have had Napoleon for six years.

"I suppose then that the ideal form of government for you would be that of the eighteenth century: the benevolent despotism of Frederick the Great perhaps?"

"Yes", he said, "Now that you mention it, I suppose it would."

Although he has been the Tenerife agent for the company since shortly after Curnow Shipping was founded, Victor Dust has never been to St. Helena - but he has had plenty to do with and for Saints travelling through Tenerife as passengers, officers or crew.

"How in your view would you sum up the nature and character of the Saints you have known - in a word?"

He hardly hesitated. "Pampered. They always seem to look to Mummy to solve their problems. They have little individual self-reliance. Perhaps it has never been allowed to develop or they have never seen the need for it. Part of the price of continuing colonial dependence, I suppose."

"Maybe that helps to explain," I said "their frustrated bafflement and continuing disbelief at being refused freedom of entry into Britain and the citizenship status accorded to the Falkland Islanders and the Gibraltarians."

"Oh, the Gibraltarians are quite different from the Saints. The Gibraltarians have known how to stand up for themselves against both the British and the Spanish Governments for years. The Saints are compliant and uncomplaining by comparison. And they don't have lobbyists."

Nor, I thought, the political clout. For the citizenship decisions in respect of both the Falkland Islands and Gibraltar had clear political and international motives. And the responses were to parliamentary pressure not unlike the half-way house quota formula which finally emerged for Hong Kong. If the *Belgrano* had taken a pot shot or two at Ladder Hill on St. Helena, things might have been different.

So 'neglected' or 'pampered'? Nigel Henry, 29 and an Assistant Purser on the *RMS*, is neither. Indeed, he has a third view.

"It is time we Saints took our own future into our own hands. We have been quiet for too long. Perhaps because we didn't know what training opportunities there were for us and how we could obtain them. My intention is to become the island's first chiropodist. I am studying chiropody now by correspondence. I don't want to stay on the ship forever, grateful as I am for the opportunity which Curnow has given me. The old people on St. Helena never wore shoes. If you look at their feet now - like those of my mother - you see that they are bleeding and sore with ingrowing toenails and bunions and deformities. And I want to do something about it.

"But if the work permit system finishes in 1994, I don't know whether I can. We are bewildered and angry about our second class status. It is like a stone in our hearts. We have this loyalty to the Crown and to Britain. But what use is loyalty if what you are loyal to denies you equality of opportunity? Denies you the very thing that your loyalty is for. No wonder we seem to lack determination and perseverance when we are not allowed to persevere where and when we want to. It's not as if thousands of us would take off for Britain. St. Helena would always be home. Once you have island life in your blood you will always want to come back."

In 1992 many Saints still display trusting naïvety, which is at first disarming and thereafter sort of worrying. Maybe it is because life in the global village has moved inexorably on; and the Saints, some say, have not. So far. But when that inherited faith, trust and acceptance begins to be questioned or challenged by the young, what then? Life in the schools is already beginning to change. The crucible for that change is there - and beyond the home. It is increasingly doubtful that it is sensible to generalise about the Saints except, arguably, in one respect.

"We Saints don't yet know how to stand up for ourselves" said one man who ought to know. "We have accepted the decisions of those in authority for too long; and assumed that decisions affecting our lives and our future cannot be influenced by our own actions and responses. The days of 'why bother' have to be numbered if we are to have any real control over our destiny. And control is, of course, only possible with responsibility and accountability."

The evening after my lunch in Santa Cruz with Victor Gonzales Dust was the last Saturday before Christmas 1991. The atmosphere outside the Hotel Atlantico was warm and welcoming. Families paraded up and down beneath the glitter of tastefully designed Christmas lights. Gentle enjoyment and civilised celebration at low key. A dais had been put up with microphones, speakers and stage lighting. The backcloth said:

> Escuela De Etnographia Y Folklore
> Patronato Municipal De Culture
> NAVIDAD MUSICAL
> En
> SANTA CRUZ

I stood for an hour and half in the crowd as groups of about twenty singers followed one another on and off the stage. They were mostly men with a few women and five or six guitars. Spanish Christmas songs, bouncing rhythm, impeccable presentation, great sound: especially from the vibrant power of the men's voices. Some up and coming Placido Domingos perhaps from Tenor Reef? *Jingle Bells* in Spanish with rhythm accompaniment was, in its way, as much of a revelation as Fats Waller. It was all done with the performers facing a McDonald's about thirty yards in front of them. Understandably, I thought, as the platform seats were duly returned to the restaurant when proceedings came to an end.

Shortly before that, a solitary African woman made stately progress through the crowds, picking her way, hips swaying, looking neither to left nor right. Her hair was in braids and on her head was the great African woman's burden: this time it was a rectangular canvas bag, the contents bursting through ancient seams. She disappeared in the crowd and I turned back to the nativity musical.

I saw her again an hour or so later. She was sitting at the side of the boulevard, her back partly resting on a post. An array of simple African crafts were laid out before her for sale. They seemed oddly out of place amid the black lace mantillas and Catholic folklorica of Spain. But she was young. There was hope in her eyes.

"What country do you come from?" I asked. She looked up, understanding, responding.

"Senegal."

"Ah. Parlez-vous francais?"

"Mais oui. Naturellement. Je suis Senegallaise."

"How long have you been in Tenerife?"

"Depuis un mois."

"I see. Bonne chance mademoiselle et bonne santé."

"Merci monsieur. Et vous aussi."

I moved away into the enveloping crowd. She had made no effort to persuade me to buy. I think of her now as I write in the pilot's cabin of the *RMS*, a day past the Equator and two days before landfall at St. Helena. Such simple human experiences are so often the best. And also so often, our minds do not perceive what our eyes try to tell us.

Nigel Henry is clearly not just a complainer. He has a 'flat top' hairdo, a brilliant smile, a logical mind and on the ship was helpfulness personified. Or purserified. Now he was reading the latest working over of Napoleon's exile on St. Helena, sitting out of uniform and alone on a rest bench beside the sea wall. Outwardly calm and reflective, the man inside is not yet at peace with himself.

"The Saints are sick and tired of so-called experts they have never heard of who come in, write some obscure report they never see, and go away again."

"True," I said. "Only too true, I'm afraid. I've been perceived as one."

"The Saints just don't care anymore about supposed developments in this or developments in that. Take education. Prince Andrew School is all very well. But the point is education for what? We go away if we are lucky for overseas training and return to derisory salaries. The gap with the expatriates is just too wide to be justified. And all the time we are thinking about our second class status in

Britain."

It was a theme I was to hear time and time again. Status. Dignity. Trust. Loyalty. Opportunity. Fairness. All the virtues that Saints understand and seek to practise in their own community. Denied them, where they historically expect to receive them, is beyond their understanding.

"We just cannot figure out how Britain can continue to let in foreigners while we in St. Helena are continually and increasingly refused access. The screw is being tightened all the time. It looks to us as if the Saints in Britain are picked on and victimised, even if they have a good job but just overstay their year a bit. All because of Hong Kong."

He smiled and the sun broke through again. "So I suppose we'll just have to keep on trying and be patient. I'm waiting for a girl but I think she has stood me up."

I wrote my recollections of our conversation an hour or so later. I had not entered into debate. The importance of what Nigel had said lay not in whether his every detail was fully accurate, or whether complex policy was fully explored. Rather, it was how he and so many other thinking Saints of a variety of ages see the issue. That is what matters - plus the deep sense of injustice that their views reflect.

Education for what? It is a constant question in any changing small island scene. The talented go away, get qualified in due expensive time, come back, expectant prophets in their own land, rediscover the pitiful money they will earn and go off again. For the island brain drain - or skills drain, is at work: not just in St. Helena, but also in Dominica, St. Lucia, Montserrat, Jamaica, Antigua, non-island Guyana, and the rest of the relatively deprived Caribbean. Cuba and Haiti may be the worst affected. The British Virgin Islands is not so badly hit, wealthy Cayman Islands almost not at all. Bermuda, also a high-salaried exception, is oceanic but not, of course, in the Caribbean.

I used to think that the brain drain from small territories reflected the ultimate financial idiocy for straitened island economies. Hard-pressed public funds are stumped up to provide three, four and six year scholarships to train professional officers to fill key posts in a Government Service. So off they go and maybe back they come to the sponsoring government or organisation with instant aspirations which do not fit comfortably with low home salaries, understaffed departments and bonded repayment of training costs if they flit.

The No. 2 in the St. Helena Legal Department is Prosecuting Officer, Registrar of Companies, Registrar of Births, Deaths and Marriages, Receiver of Wreck etc. etc.

"You name it" he says "I do it." Alan Nicholls is personable, presentable and apparently experienced - but unqualified. And perhaps by now in that respect demotivated, since his two attempts to qualify in law have been unsuccessful. As the so-called Legal Officer of St. Helena, he earned a salary of less than £6,000.

"The Attorney General, my boss, is an expatriate with £30,000. I love my job, but the difference is hard to bear sometimes. Our last salary increase was over three years ago."

I remembered many years ago in colonial Fiji, the first Fijian M.A. in education complaining bitterly:

"When I objected to a promotion block for me, they said I wasn't qualified. So I went away, in those pioneering days, got qualified and a step beyond. I came back and said 'There you are, what next?' They said 'Ah, you may be qualified now, but you lack experience. Sorry. Wait your turn.' 'Did that' I asked 'apply to young administrative officers straight from Oxford?' 'Oh', was the reply 'that's different.'"

He was a thorn in the flesh of an insensitive colonial government forever after and ended up an aggressive near-alcoholic at the UN, post-independence in 1970.

So, it may seem, *La Ronde Educationelle* achieves nothing. But we have to take a more liberal view or sink into inertia and negativism. What has been given to those successfully trained but who leave is the opportunity to gain professional experience, acceptance and reward in a wider environment and in a bigger world. Their island of origin can take pride in that; and recognise that those who achieve success elsewhere carry their country and people and inheritance with them. St. Helena should not, I believe, bemoan the fact that they go, after a bit; or do not return at all for the time being. They are not 'lost' to St. Helena in a broad sense. The nomadic instinct runs with isolation. The call of home will prevail when they - and the island - are ready; but re-assimilation is no simple or easy process.

'Education for what' then is perhaps a little clearer. And the price to pay for it is the expensive engagement of short-term transit camp expatriates, sometimes escaping from other developing countries. *La Ronde Educationelle* is inescapable.

I have met Pakistanis and Jamaicans in Britain who refuse to go to other than a Pakistani or Jamaican lawyer or doctor. The Saints in St. Helena and in Britain might think about that.

*   *   *

There was yet another view to be found on the *RMS*. Nick Thorpe, son and heir of a prominent trading and landed family in St. Helena, was travelling home from England with two growing children. He is good looking and personable if somewhat shy and self-protective. He did not seem to mix with or talk to the other Saints with any degree of spontaneity or enthusiasm. Maybe money divided.

"St. Helena," he said "is the prima donna of the British South Atlantic. All the others - Tristan, The Falklands and Ascension - seem to be able to make a go of it economically, but not St. Helena. Its economy and life style are, of course, saved - bailed out for the time being - by the employment of about 250 Saints in the Falklands and maybe 800, including families, in Ascension. Their remittances home suffice to build a house in stages - each room represents a year on Ascension you could say. But they come back old men, worn out at 55 from the booze..."

"The Saints pull down those who succeed. There is a story - apocryphal I suppose - about an Indian merchant who set up a business to export live crabs. He did so in boxes without lids.

'Why do you do this?' he was asked, 'Surely the crabs will climb out at the top of the box and escape.'

'Not at all,' replied the merchant. 'Each time a crab tries to get out at the top of the box, the others below will drag him back. So no crab can ever escape. They are all kept down, and I save money on box lids.'

"That's a bit like the Saints," said Nick Thorpe, speaking from the heart of inherited or personal experience, it would seem, as he plunged with his children into the ship's swimming pool. The South Sahara sand and haze were no longer over the ship. We were abreast of Liberia. A solitary great kamikaze locust crashed down on the deck. An understandable urge to escape, I thought. Like those crabs.

Victor Gonzales Dust came aboard the *RMS* when she docked again at Santa Cruz de Tenerife at 0500 on Friday, 14th February 1992 on Voyage 6 North. He accompanied Andrew Bell and his wife Prue, plus a Jewish-American Indian, prosaically named Sanford Smith, to Tenerife airport.

He it was who told me that the story of the crabs is an ancient American Indian tale of wisdom. He had known of it for at least thirty years. So do such tales cross cultures, for there is nothing new in the world of philosophy.

Victor returned to the ship for a breakfast of Scots porridge, his favourite non-available delight for that time of day. He left at 11 a.m. clutching a large ice cream carton filled with English scones baked by Saints on the ship. These were the modest and unexpected indulgences of a former French Consul in a Spanish territory who was the devoted agent of a British registered ship. Perhaps that is what constitutes a true European.

CHAPTER 4

Officers and Passengers

If Agatha Christie had written *Murder on the RMS St. Helena*, she could hardly have contrived to put together a more fascinating collection of passengers and circumstances.

"This ship is so full of intrigue, it is difficult to know what and who to believe," said one British officer, which I, eavesdropping and sitting innocently in a deck chair, found equally difficult to believe. There were, however, some serious undercurrents, carefully kept from the passengers. Curnow Shipping had won the contract to run the St. Helena Service in 1977. When the announcement was made in the House of Commons in 1986 of the Thatcher government's decision to build a new ship, it was stated that Curnow would continue to run the old ship until it was replaced, would be associated with the design and construction of the new ship and be retained as its managing operators and agents for three years after it was put into service. Continuity at that stage was king. Thereafter everything would be up for grabs again by public tender.

So far so good; but later ODA thought it prudent to engage consultants to advise it on future management and operational tenders. The three year shakedown period began to be whittled away. First it was necessary to disengage or be distanced from the existing managers. To this end therefore officers - not crew who signed on and off per voyage - both British and St. Helenian, had to be given notice of termination of employment. This was done by individual letters which awaited everyone on their arrival in St. Helena from Ascension in January, 1992. They were all given three months notice. Reactions were understandably bitter and confused.

There had been other problems before this. "There is simmering discontent among the crew," Myron Benjamin told me. As Second Engineer, he was one of the two most senior Saints on board. Quiet and reserved at first with a black handlebar moustache, he was a classic example of still waters running deep. Although qualified to be Chief Engineer, he was not restive about his position - yet.

"The discontent is not between the Saint officers and the British officers. The crew is beginning to feel exploited. Goodwill and courtesy remain on the surface, but hurt and resentment is building up underneath."

I asked why.

"The British officers mainly do a one-on, one-off schedule of voyages. Most Saints do two-on and one-off. This is not fair. I personally get on well with most of the British officers; but some, maybe a few - I name no names - are patronising and unsympathetic or disinterested in us. Or so it seems. I look forward to the day when the captain and officers are all Saints; but we have to be patient until then. The company won't listen to us. They don't want to know how we feel. They have their own ideas."

He paused, smiled and looked up.

"You mustn't pay too much attention to me. And neither should the company. I was just letting off a bit of steam. Quite appropriate for an engineer, I suppose."

Rumours flourished on the voyage, as rumours do in the closeted atmosphere of a passenger carrying ship.

"I suppose you know all about what's going on," said the ship's surgeon unexpectedly on the sun deck one afternoon.

"No I don't," I replied, accurately, but apparently unconvincingly.

"Well if you don't, you no doubt soon will." He made no effort to expand on this cryptic observation and moved away.

The officers were clearly pre-occupied. Those directly involved in passenger relations did their best but with no manifest relish for their task.

"I hear that this may be the last voyage of the ship under its present management" announced a mountain-climbing ex-Zimbabwean agriculturalist.

"Oh" I said, disbelief in my voice.

"The new airport on St. Helena will presumably make it redundant. Anyway that's what I believe."

"I hardly think so - even if there conceivably could be an airport. The new ship has only just gone into service. Its task is to serve and service St. Helena: passengers, cargo and mail. The last Royal Mail Ship."

"Oh yes. I suppose that must be right. Well, you know what ships like this are like: alive with rumours."

"Do I? Then you should ignore them." I sounded schoolmasterly and prim.

One of the things ships are not is the carrier with any degree of frequency of the co-founder of the *Guinness Book of Records*. One day Norris McWhirter went public to the passengers of the *RMS St. Helena*.

"It all began," he said "with a phone call in 1954 and as a book to settle arguments in pubs and college dining rooms." He took it initially to W.H. Smith. The chief buyer agreed to take six copies on a sale or return basis. Nearly forty years later, it has gone rather further than that. It was quickly a best seller and has remained so ever since. It is now published in 39 languages and is run from Enfield by a team of 55. There were 8,000 entries in the first edition; now 15,000. About 22% of the entries change from one annual edition to the next.

"It is an arduous business being a chronicler of records" says McWhirter. Sales to date are in excess of 69 million copies. This, he claims, is equivalent to 18 stacks each as high as Mt. Everest. Who am I to question that? It is a favoured birthday present - and every day in the United Kingdom 162,000 people have birthdays. Not everyone obtains it that way; the *Guinness Book of Records* is in its own book as the most frequently stolen library book.

Landfall at St. Helena was thirty six hours away. I stood at the rail of the *RMS* watching a burnished sun sink into oblivion. I had come out of the cabin wearing a Fijian *sulu* round my waist.

"Into your fancy dress already, are you?" asked an ageing Colonel from Tunbridge Wells. (Actually, all ageing Colonels live in Tunbridge Wells - or Budleigh Salterton.)

"Not exactly. Just my usual evening domestic garment that I relax in, irrespective of climate."

He looked at me unbelievingly and passed by; then turned to his wife.

"Curious people you find on passenger ships these days. Standards slipping yet again. Very sad really. Coloured skirts for old men. Extraordinary."

* * *

Shortly after one o'clock each afternoon at sea, the public address system sprang into life. It did so as usual next day for School Bus and his sitrep announcement.

"This is the officer of the watch speaking. Here are the main navigational details for 29th December, 1991. At noon today the ship was 270 nautical miles nor' nor' west of St. Helena. We expect to arrive at James Bay at approximately 9 a.m. tomorrow morning. The depth of water beneath the vessel at this point is 5,763 feet."

"Good God," exploded the retired agriculturalist from Zimbabwe as he placed a pre-Christmas *Daily Telegraph* carefully beside his deckchair. "Why do they have to give us all that stuff about the depth of water. I would have thought that all they needed to do is to confirm each day that the water beneath the ship is sufficient." I spread the story. The idea apparently caught on. Once anyway. Just north of Cape Finisterre on the voyage home and in twelve feet rolling swells, Cadet Robert Huxtable did the daily announcement of the ship's progress on behalf of officer of the watch Second Mate School Bus. At the end he said, deadpan:

..."and the depth of the water beneath the ship is such that we don't have to worry about it!" The captain had apparently sanctioned - perhaps suggested - it, a sense of humour happily alive. I don't think many passengers noticed. Most were comatose anyway. Except the

Saints.

Every afternoon, the young Saints were on the sun deck, ghetto blaster at full throttle. St. Helena - and no doubt love as well - was just around the corner.

"Is the favourite music on the island still country and western?" I asked.

"Yeah. But I don' like that."

"What do you like?"

"Oh, rock, hard rock, soft rock, pineapple rock." He had blacked-out glasses, Bermuda shorts with a snake pattern, a rounded beard and tattoos on both arms. "Concrete blues. Soul."

"Reggae?"

"Yeah reggae. Anything like that. What you goin' to do on St. Helena? You come to spy on us?"

"Not exactly."

"You been there before?"

"Yes. Twice."

"Why you came then?"

"I came for the Overseas Development Administration," I confessed. "You know - ODA. On what's rather grandly called a BAR mission. Budgetary Aid Review."

"Oh that. I hear o' that. So you're an ODA spy, not just any spy. What ODA ever do for St. Helena? Just come out, lie on the ship, walk aroun', waste time, waste money, chat up our girls, go back on the ship, nothin' ever happen. Bad goes, worse come. That what we say. What you spy on this time?"

"Can't tell you yet. When I've finished my spying, I'll send you a copy of my report so you can comment on it."

"That's good. I can do that. I been at Oxford for six years."

The others dissolved in laughter. "At Oxford! Big University man with big mout'. What you got? Second Class degree in Rock an' Roll or somethin'?"

"Say," he said to me. "You know that Colonel Haw Haw over there. He came up an' complain to us 'bout our music. Went inside to see some British officer. He come out and say 'Please boys turn the music down a bit. The Colonel can't sleep in his sun chair.' What you think o' that, spy man?"

"Well," I said, "why didn't you tell him that you are happy. You are nearly home. You are outside on the sun deck. And whose ship is it anyway?"

He looked at me, mouth open. "Boy, that the right answer. I didn' t'ink o' that. Let me shake you hand. You can stay and spy as long as you like on St. Helena. I got a piece o' land I wan' to sell. You like to buy it?"

CHAPTER 5

When the Saints ...

'St. Helenians are of mixed origin,' says the handout in stylised understatement, 'being descended from British settlers sent out by the East India Company and from company employees and slaves from the South Asian Sub-continent, the East Indies and Madagascar, as well as a small number of Chinese and Africans.'

Cynthia Bennett, married to the head of the St. Helena Customs Department, was 34 and one of a family of ten children. She is short, demure, pale-skinned with gleaming white teeth and a slow beguiling smile. There are two young children and a new house, the fruits of four years working for Pan Am on Ascension Island in her case; and eighteen years there in the case of husband Dougie.

"The people I worked for were wonderful. That was what made it almost bearable. But we had to live the whole time in just one room - you've seen the kind of thing - and if we wanted some space we had to go outside. I was so homesick. Ascension has no roots, no culture, no traditions, no soul. I hated it, but it was the sacrifice we had to make, like so many other Saints, to be able to afford, rather quickly, a house and now a family. I've not been anywhere else; and I don't want to be anywhere else but St. Helena. I am happy here. I am fulfilled."

A family like hers exemplified the heterogeneous racial inheritance of the Saints. Brothers and sisters can differ widely in appearance, hair and face colour, physique and features. Of the dining saloon stewards on the ship, one looked Indonesian, one Italian, one Micronesian, one straight Devon, one Spanish, one Afro-Caribbean, one Chinese-Polynesian. One older man might conceivably have been Latin-American Indian. Yet they all come from St. Helena. The only genetical individual common denominator is being uncommon.

It is arguably the greatest human quality - cohesive variety - that an isolated community can possess. The snobbery of colour is so rare as to be virtually non-existent; the awareness of difference is non-attitudinal. Each new baby is a surprise re-jigging of the genes. Pride is in belonging to St. Helena; not competing with others over gradations of skin colour and features.

"When we came out of Cardiff," said one of the deck stewards, "half the crew were suck."

The distorted pronunciation of the letter 'i' is a characteristic of Saints' speech. Sixpence becomes suckspence. It is not altogether unlike what happens to the same letter in New Zealand where 'milk' is 'moolk' and 'tea' is 'toy'. Or nearly so. In a burst of passing affection, one old lady said to me, 'Giv us a kuss, luv.' There are other variants, of course, one being the frequent interchange or confusion between v and w. The Saints share this with both the Pitcairners and the Tristanians. Perhaps it all goes back to common roots in England where in some counties it has been said 'they can't tell the difference between a wee and a wubbleyew.'

In spite of their isolation and limited contact with outside influences, the Saints are prone to all the common ailments. Indeed a British researcher who studied the problem a few years ago concluded that St. Helena has the highest per capita incidence of diabetes in the world.

When I was on the island for that short period in late 1986, I stayed at Seaview which is a Government-owned bungalow high in the hills above Jamestown. It is commonly known at the Judge's Lodge because the non-resident Chief Justice stays there when he comes to preside over the Supreme Court sitting once or twice a year. Every morning there was a stream of young women walking by on their way down the hill to work. Almost without exception at that time of year, they wheezed and spluttered with asthma or hay fever.

On the voyage south of the *RMS*, officers, crew and passengers had been progressively afflicted by a wretched kind of influenza. It did not remain just on the ship. In the 24th January issue of *St. Helena News*, the Chief Medical Officer lamented:

'In addition to its usual cargo, the *RMS St. Helena* recently delivered a flu-like viral infection to the island. Very many adults and children have been affected. The symptoms include fever, cough, headaches, sore throat, muscle aches and pains and fatigue ...'

The Fatal Impact at work yet again on an island people, sufficiently serious a week later, for all schools to be closed as pupils and teachers alike succumbed in scores. In fact 'hundreds,' the Chief Education Officer, Basil George, told me.

If you are at all like me, you will be constantly intrigued by the wide perceptual differences of the same thing by apparently similar people. I spoke with two mid-life Saints, male and bright, as to how they viewed their homeland. One was a passenger. He was returning after a brief period in Britain. The second was an experienced and long-serving dining saloon steward, widely travelled and about to enjoy a few months leave at home in St. Helena.

"If you had to sum up in one word" I asked them together "your perceptions of St. Helena today, what would that word be?"

"Chaos," said the returning resident without hesitation.

"Paradise" said the steward. We all laughed. Both were surprised, it seemed.

"Tell me," I asked the first. "Explain."

"It's the Government! There doesn't seem to be any real direction or leadership. A succession of expatriates come and go at the Castle, each cancelling or abandoning what the one before started; dragging the Saints in different directions; and then leaving the mess to someone else who comes in and the Saints discover that we know more than he does."

"About what?"

"Oh about farming and agriculture and forestry and construction and what is sensible and what is stupid, I suppose. For us on St. Helena. They learn from us most often, not the other way round. And they are paid enormous salaries and our people get nothing or nearly nothing. Even the Councillors seem out of touch. You should talk to the people. They know. They see the expats meeting only each other most of the time, eating Ann's fishcakes, drinking Castle beer and complaining about everything. And their wives are even worse in those houses on Piccolo Hill. Why they come to live with us I don't understand. They should stay home in England."

"I see what you mean," said the second Saint. "All that may be true. But I am going back soon to set up business because there are great opportunities for us Saints if only we can take them. There is so much that can be done. Don't wait and expect the Government to do it. Most things the Government does are a mess - like the fisheries development. Money wasted - nothing achieved. And yet to have a successful tuna canning industry we have to bring in an expatriate. Why can't we do it ourselves? Anyway I'm going to try. And it **is** a paradise compared to other places. There may be a fight or two occasionally when the boys get a bit drunk. But there are no knives, no drugs, no muggings and no robbery. You can still leave your house open when you go out and not lock your car. Try that in England and see what happens."

It was Boxing Day, 1991. I had been reading *The Independent* of Sunday 15th December. **'STABBING WAS 60TH THIS YEAR'** said the headline: the sixtieth knife attack on unarmed police officers in London in 1991. Two died.

The *RMS* was due in James Bay on the morning of 30th December. There would certainly be chaos on shore then - wonderful warming exciting chaos, the chaos of arrival, horns tooting from creaking trucks. Stumping up the slippery landing steps and into the arms of friends and relatives and counting the boxes and arguing with Customs and opening them all at home and " ... just look what I brought **you** - from England."

Then real goat curry for New Year - after a Castle beer or two at the Consulate.

CHAPTER 6

The Landing

Just as there are islands and islands, so there are landings and landings. The *RMS* anchors off-shore in James Bay in the shadow of those awesome, stark, brown, craggy, formidably steep and unwelcoming cliffs. The colours change as the day goes on; but the menace is always there and there is no relief as you view them from the ship or on shore.

The seas run along the protecting wall, fizzing up high and fast. When that water moves, it moves. A ferry service of small boats runs the homing passengers ashore, clutching their TVs and videos and Hi Fi's. They know what to expect before they reach the soil - or stone - of St. Helena again. For the stranger, it is different of course. The little boats sweep left in a gentle ark, depending on the state of the sea. Then they edge slowly in stern first to a tiny landing twenty feet plus across, three sets of steps, the bottom covered in green slime. Above the steps attached to a horizontal stanchion are five ropes about four feet apart. As your boat lifts and the stern bangs against the steps, you leap as boat and steps come abreast, grasp hold of a rope and pull yourself ashore. If you are wise you get off that slimey step fast. Not everyone succeeds. Even Governors. One anyway: when he waited, in white uniform, sword and plumed hat, to clasp the hand of Prince Andrew as he too grabbed a rope and leapt ashore at the Jamestown Landing in 1984. The Governor went down a step too far, his foot flirted with the slime and the bottom half of His Uniformed Excellency slid momentarily beneath the surface of an angry sea. It was one of the richest minor moments for British television and placed St. Helena fleetingly, and for entirely the wrong reason, in the consciousness of the British public. It is the best argument I know for the abolition of an anachronistic Gilbert and Sullivan costume.

First to board the *RMS* when the anchor and the gangway have been lowered are the Harbour Master, Customs Officers, Police and Immigration officials of the Government of the Crown Colony of St. Helena. Each landing passenger is interviewed, his or her intentions established and passport stamped. Non-St. Helenians contribute £5 per head to the coffers of an impecunious administration. Saints pay nothing - arguably inequitable dispensation, except to the returning Saints. A neatly written receipt is passed over, together with a landing card for presentation to a police constable at the gangway as evidence of the payment. I should have thought that the receipt would suffice - especially since the constable on duty when I went ashore showed no interest in collecting my landing card. Maybe it was because I had taken the precaution of leaving with the Senior Customs Officer.

A visitor also receives what is described as an Immigration Permit which requires him to advise the Governor about all sorts of things. Useful I suppose if you are yearning for that all-important printed invitation with the crown on it and you change your address. Then, as one of the conditions of the permit, it says what seems to be a prohibition on underwater breathing:

> 'The holder of this permit shall deposit all underwater breathing appara-
> tus with the Immigration Officer. The apparatus shall be returned to the
> holder when he leaves St. Helena or may be returned to him temporarily
> whilst he remains in St. Helena subject to such conditions as may be
> specified by the Immigration Officer.'

Such as not using it underwater, I suppose. And another thing - if by any chance you have secreted on your person any cargo or other articles belonging to a ship which has been wrecked on the coasts of St. Helena and fail to hand over what it is you have secreted on your person, oh boy, you will be up against the law of the land.

There is an alternative method of getting ashore. This is how

Curnow Shipping describes it:

Dear Passenger,

LANDING FACILITIES AT ST. HELENA

We draw your attention to the fact that Jamestown has no facility for the *RMS ST. HELENA* to berth alongside a quay or wharf. All passengers therefore embark and disembark at St. Helena by licensed launches via the wharf steps and the ship's gangway.

For those passengers who are unable to negotiate comfortably either the gangway or the wharf steps, arrangements can be made for them to be landed in a specially-adapted cargo box which is lowered over the ship's side into a lighter and subsequently lifted from there directly on to the wharf.

When I first revealed this at Sevenoaks in 1985, there was a burst of instant laughter at the geriatric vista which it apparently presented. I thought the idea rather inviting, not least when on 30th December, 1991, I saw the arriving Chief Justice and his wife gently lowered over the side of the ship in a contraption which bore some resemblance to a 1927 open-air skilift cabin. It was picked up by a shore crane at the receiving end and safely delivered with its passengers on to the landing. No doubt a message reporting the first part

of a judicial mission judiciously accomplished without imperilling the life insurance policy then went off to the right slot in the FCO.

Labour on board, flotilla of cargo lighters around the ship, entry formalities complete, I went ashore. That is to say I went down the gangway and successfully negotiated the rise and fall of the small open boat whose task it was to convey me and others to the landing. There awaiting us was that soccer goal post-like stanchion with its five ropes dangling down from the crossbar. Then the steps below: the slimey three leading to a sort of half-way house platform, eight dry ones to safety above. The boat rose in the petulant swell to slimey step two. I stepped bravely forth - in my sixty-ninth year - grasped a rope, pulled and slithered up to safe ground. So far so good. Now to run the gauntlet of the assembled Saints of indeterminate age who scrutinise each landing passenger with the critical skill of all island-ers. Freed from all official involvements and responsibilities, I would look anew at the island of St. Helena: forbidding, of epic grandeur and dynamic contrasts. I would talk, without restraint, to its gentle, courteous, discerning people. And hopefully, they too with me. I would ... An old man sitting with others inside the customs zone fixed me with a straight stare, supported apparently by a tediously long memory.

"You come to spy on us again for ODA?" he postulated to the St. Helenian world.

It was not really a question. Just the same jolting judgement as on the *RMS*. You can't fool island people. They know all about you before you know it yourself. Good grief, I was labelled, packed, disposed of - all over the island - before I had even begun: The Spy Who Came In From The Ship.

"No. Not for ODA. Not this time. Just ..." I paused. Just ... For myself? For the Saints? For St. Helena? Too pretentious all that. It was a question I couldn't comfortably answer. Spying, I suppose, yes. In a sense. But for whom and for what? Old Islanders know a thing or two. Indeed they do. And, not for the first time, I should have to remember that.

CHAPTER 7

New Year's Day

I met the Colonel from you-know-where in Main Street. Most shipboard passengers recognise one another instantly in the mecca of their odyssey. They do so at times with reserve, even distaste, not always well concealed. Close shipboard familiarity does breed that thing.

"You are still here then?" he asked.

"Yes."

"I thought you had been deported to Ascension."

"It seems not."

"So I see. Pity." He walked aimlessly on to Solomons, the Consulate, the Star, The Emporium, the Freemasons' Hall, the Jehovahs' Witnesses and the Free Foresters. He looked at none. He was entirely without curiosity. We had passed each other at the annual New Year's Day festivity for school children at Prince Andrew School on Francis Plain. It was midday. The Chevy charabanc was due to leave at four: far too late for those who had lost interest after half an hour in the morning.

"God, how slowly the time is going" he said. And padded on.

Down below in the great terraced sports field with the vast blue Atlantic as a spectacular backdrop, families from all over St. Helena had assembled for their special sports competition day. It was relaxed fun, splendidly organised; marred by nothing: innocent community pleasure free from yobbos, drunks, slobs, aggression and, at that stage, garbage - all those things that the Colonel should have seen and recognised and welcomed. Yet he did not - like others when faced with innocent beguiling pleasure which they find they no longer understand.

Joy George, the Acting Head, found time to take the incoming Administrator of Tristan da Cunha, his wife and me over the new Prince Andrew School. And what an impressive institution it is: well-stocked library, science laboratories, computer and typing rooms, school orchestra rehearsal studio and private practice music booths, tuckshop and staffrooms, multi-purpose assembly hall for indoor sports, stage shows, examinations and community centre. Cost corners may have been cut; but the school buildings, on the drawing board only when I had last been in St. Helena in 1986, are there in splendid staggered formation overlooking a spacious sports arena and the Atlantic Ocean. There are 46 teachers for 400 pupils, a ratio of which any open school in Britain would be proud to achieve. Seventy per cent of the courses are vocational.

Suddenly I found Cynthia Bennett. Or rather, in the massed crowds, she spotted me, the stranger, as I was about to pass by.

"I've just been shown over the school by the Acting Head, Joy George."

"Ah," said Cynthia. "And what did you think?"

"Great. Splendid. First two A level successes who have gone right through the school system are now in England."

"Just as well you think that." She smiled that slow subtle smile.

"Why?"

"She's my sister."

"Oh God," I said. "One of the ten."

"Yes."

The people of island communities steal up on you and knock you sideways with their surprises when you are stupid enough to open your mouth. Those of St. Helena do it more gently than some and with an engaging sense of mild amusement at your discomfort. Cynthia is a polished exponent of this Saintly skill.

"What are you doing tomorrow?" she asked me.

"I'm starting with Cable and Wireless. Going to The Briars to see the manager, George Stevens."

"That's good."

"Why?"

"He's my brother-in-law."

"I suppose you're going to tell me that you are a relation of the

Governor's wife."

"No I'm not."

"Why?"

"Because I'm not."

"Well, that's a relief." We both laughed.

"Dougie?" I asked. "Where's he?" There were two babies in close proximity but no husband.

"He's home. Been vomiting all night and still suck. Can't think why."

"So you're here alone. I suppose they will say you left him sick at home in order to meet a bald-headed old passenger from the *RMS* on Francis Plain."

"You sure got us right" said a woman of about 40 who had overheard me. Now she hopped from leg to leg with excitement.

"You got the Saints off. That what we gonna say 'bout Cyntie - and Dougie home suck."

A retired bank branch manager approached us.

"It is four o'clock. The others are waiting in the charabanc."

"Yes" I said reluctantly. "I suppose it is and they are."

I had arranged the transportation and had been first on board at 10 a.m. The others arrived at desultory intervals up to half an hour later.

The 18-seater 1929 Chevrolet charabanc, registered number 82, is a minor institution on St. Helena. It has no doors and no roof covering, apart from a sort of canvas-like canopy stacked at the back. The seats are, well, basic wooden with massive applications of tape like a decrepit antediluvian suitcase. Cecil Corker owns. Son Colin Corker drives, hand on the horn. The old lady has been in the family since 1950, together with a 1932 Bedford truck and a 1939 Ford V8.

I clambered aboard at three minutes past four to disapproving looks all round.

"You'll be late for the second resurrection," said a surly Liverpudlian with a face like an over-ripe tomato and a cloth cap on his head. He wore it in the ship's lounges and carried it with him to the dining saloon. His name was Arthur. He seemed to have no other.

As we rode back up and round and looked down on a still pulsating Francis Plain, I pondered the question as to why cranky old people come to a divine community and fail to notice, let alone respond to, what it offers them. Perhaps it is because it makes them uneasy. Their normal reaction is one of criticism which gives them a superior pleasure. When they find nothing of substance to criticise, they are unhappy and petulant. So why indeed do they want to come, cheque books out, in the first place?

No one can be sure. To see themselves, in the case of the couple at the back of the charabanc, in the *Guinness Book of Records* and those of their Travellers' Century Club of Los Angeles as the most travelled pairing ever - based on countries visited globe-wise. To them, their sole objective was to set foot on Tristan da Cunha and go back with the evidence. They would have clocked up three hundred and five of whatever places that counted and live content in the delusion of such 'achievement'. So they regaled with delight the rigours of getting out to their ship from Pitcairn; or going ashore in the British Antarctic or Punta Arenas. To them St. Helena was of no essential interest other than the personally statistical: two chimerical Flying Dutchmen bent on going on and on and on ...

... I returned to the *RMS*, riding proudly in a calm James Bay. Another glorious sunset, the first for 1992, was beginning. It had been a wonderful peoples' day, now to be crowned in visual splendour. On such an evening, St. Helena is one of the island jewels of the ocean world. What Saints take for granted the rest of the world yearns for: calm, peace, security, kinship, clean unpolluted air, pure water and, in the main, fulfilment. Long may their forbidding cliffs and oceanic isolation keep a degraded world out. It was time for that sort of wish on New Year's Day.

A month later I went again to Francis Plain to watch a club cricket match. One side was captained by Patrick Joshua, the licensee and manager of the Consulate Hotel. On the other was the ship's officers cabin steward on Voyage 6 South until he slipped the ship at St.

Helena. He was now a barman at the hotel.

I don't quite know why a cricket match on a rocky fortress island in the South Atlantic should seem strange. But it did, not least because I had decided to have fun and put on my MCC tie. Perhaps it was a first ever appearance at a South Atlantic island cricket match. I picked up a bat and practised a few long unused shots. Then hit a ball or two with unnerving lack of skill. I went out into the middle and bowled an over at unguarded stumps. Hit none, as my body protested. I ran to catch a high return from the boundary, took it on the full, held it and decided to retire for the last time. It was like climbing the 699 steps of Jamestown's Jacob's Ladder and coming down again in 1986. Once was enough.

Someone had a portable radio tuned to the BBC World Service Saturday afternoon sports programme. It was the last minutes of the commentary on the Wales v France rugby union match at Cardiff Arms Park ... 'And at Twickenham, England is running up a cricket score against Ireland 38-9 ...' Well, not quite a cricket score, but more than enough.

The Saints were watching their side batting in St. Helena and listening to Five Nations rugby in Britain. It was somehow symbolic, but odd. One game they don't play on St. Helena is rugby football.

"Don't forget to send us some equipment," they said as I left. "That county side in Kent must have lots of good bats and pads they don't use any more. Send them to the Fire Station in Jamestown."

"I'll try," I said. "I'll try. I've done it once for Tonga. Let me try to do it for St. Helena."

CHAPTER 8

Fallibility

Have you ever attempted to encapsulate in words the qualities and characteristics that make a country and people distinctive and different? Well, in October 1985, I had a shot at summarising my sweet-and-sour reactions to a first footing on the soil of St. Helena. Since this is confession time, here is a piece I wrote then - for critical examination eight years later.

A visit to the island of St. Helena is a return to the 19th century. An isolated South Atlantic imperial fortress, its unwelcoming, craggy cliffs yield beyond to soft, green mountainous grasslands and valleys. The capital, Jamestown, is a miniature Andorra, nestling narrowly and alone between towering, rock-studded hills. The island is 1,600 miles from the Cape of Good Hope and 700 miles from Ascension Island. A signpost points wistfully to London, where the hearts of all true 'Saints' lie, some 5,600 oceanic miles north.

High in the mountains beyond Jamestown, the Governor's residence of Plantation House is a sumptuous Georgian mansion with breathtaking dominance of land and sea; and with resplendent Queen Anne furniture. And old-world splendour pervades its 46 rooms. Governors preside with a sense of uneasy anachronism and one at least with the intellectual range of a country squire. The BBC World Service does little to relieve the inward-looking social incestuousness that only a remote island community can both nurture and sustain.

The outside world emerges briefly every 6-8 weeks with the arrival of the 3,500 ton *RMS St. Helena*. It is virtually the sole physical link with the outside world. Together with a small fuel carrier, the *Bosun Bird*, the vessel is subsidised to the extent of £2,300,000 per annum by the United Kingdom Government: and brings in cargo and passengers (76). There is no airstrip and no prospect of one. There is a reasonably good telex service, but a shaky telephone link via Ascension Island. These are the sole concessions to modern communications technology. Sadly, the capital cost and the low traffic level do not warrant a major face-lift for one of Cable & Wireless's oldest and historically most interesting of services.

The people of St. Helena are an eye-catching blend of Asian, Chinese,

African and European strains. Their demure rustic charm has long since gone from other more worldly lands. Mothers of 15 and 16 are far from uncommon. It is easy to see why. 'Spares,' as they are called, abound. 'Good morning, sir' the children say as they smile at you in the streets.

The policies of the Government of St. Helena are largely in the hands of an oligarchy of three expatriate civil servants - the Governor, the Government Secretary, and the Colonial Treasurer. They are, as one would expect, far from career front-runners. The word ' innovatory' does not appear in their verbal dictionaries; but 'we must not rock the boat' does. Frequently. They respond to situations often with misgivings or reluctance; and do not seem capable of anticipating the problems that clearly lie ahead. The fact is that the outside world is slowly but inexorably catching up with St. Helena. This may be a great pity, but it cannot be brushed aside. Escape routes to the United Kingdom and South Africa are closed. Unemployment is rife and a degree of social unrest may be imminent..

Among the people of St. Helena, there is a similar but community-wide conservatism, more deep-seated than any I have experienced elsewhere; and to date less pressure, none of it being political, for change of any major kind. For example, the Crown Agents are seen by the Saints as an arm of a British government from whom all goodies come - not least being the 75% grant in aid towards annual recurrent expenditure. There would thus be no political support for severing Crown Agents connections; and any such proposal would be received locally with distrust and concern. It would be seen as indicating 'abandonment' by London; and would sound alarm bells in Westminster and Jamestown...

There are some things still right and some that are now wrong with that past attempt at instant analysis and judgement in respect of St. Helena. I was entirely mistaken about the bleak future of telecommunications. The ever-resourceful Clive Warren encouraged (his word in Diplomatic Speak) Cable & Wireless to provide a vastly improved service to St. Helena. And so they should, I thought when I heard. Commercial considerations are not everything. Or so it must be argued with conviction from time to time in matters of this kind.

I may yet be proved mistaken - although I hope not - about an airport. There is a relatively new (1988) Constitution with increased, although far from complete, decision-making power in the hands of the elected Councillors. There is less oligarchic sterility and now a government of increasing purposefulness and planning. Although it exists, unemployment is not now rife; and social unrest is not now imminent. We shall see why this is so. There is far less conservatism *per se* than seven years ago; and wider and more varied opinions and debates about the future of St. Helena and its people. There have been some healthy and some less healthy developments in social and family life. Mothers of 15 and 16 are no longer, I was assured, 'far from uncommon.' Better and earlier sex education, plus fear of AIDS, may help to explain this. There is still suspicion of cliquey expats and their silly 'Thank God It's Bloody Friday'(TGIBF) tie. But there is now a man at work at the top who, with his wife, has a short fuse for this sort of schoolboy insensitivity on the part of contract officialdom ...

Now read on.

CHAPTER 9

Change

'There is nothing more difficult to take in hand, nor perilous to conduct, or more uncertain of its success, than the introduction of a new order of things, because the innovator has for enemies all those who have done well under the old conditions, and lukewarm defenders in those who may do well - but don't yet know - under the new.'

Thus Machiavelli, an impatient architect of change and loved the less because of it.

A much earlier and cynically different view of change was that of a retrospective Caius Petronius Arbiter, Roman satirist of the first century A.D.

'I was to learn later in life that we tend to meet any new situation by reorganising; and a wonderful method it can be for creating the illusion of progress while producing confusion, inefficiency and demoralisation.'

This is not what is wanted in some countries you will readily call to mind. It is the substance, not the shadow, of change in public life for which their people yearn.

*   *   *

Just as there are islands and islands, so there are governors and governors - one impatient for change like Machiavelli, but not always for the right things or for the right reasons; another socially indolent, an increasingly drink-prone Arbiter. Some care; some tick off the days on the calendar until the hallelujah date of release from thraldom. Some have flair and sensitivity for the feelings and frustrations of those over whose territory they temporarily preside. These rare ones achieve acceptance and thus trust, at which point they are removed - for their own good it is sometimes said gently to them. 'Going native' is the ultimate diplomatic transgression for Whitehall. Less forgivable than either incompetence or indolence. Some indulge, while others suffer from, the social arrogance and uxorious banalities of cultural misfits, who in due course pass into unlamented oblivion.

Not only colonial governors and their ladies, of course. Many 'second eleven' expatriates have fallen into the same trap. Bored to crocodile tears, all their wives do is lament their misfortunes to others similarly inclined and proclaim the intolerable limitations of the 'locals' well into the tropical night. The tree frogs and crickets echo their endless protestations.

The fact is - sad or otherwise - that there is no longer any directly related career base from which those who go to fill dependent territory posts are drawn. The Colonial Service and all its ways may long since have gone out of favour and into history. But whatever its limitations, it did provide a cadre of career experience over many decades. Now both the experience has gone and, seemingly, the virtue or value of it too. Apart from the world of diplomacy and perhaps development, not any more is a period of overseas service from Britain regarded as public service career enhancement. Rather, it can be those masters of mediocrity who, with a firm grasp of the obvious, opt for a three year term with a grand title in a small dependent territory. There the exceptions will learn more - if they have the humility - from those self-same 'locals' than they ever would in Bradford or Cirencester or Sutton. Or, I should with total impartiality add, in Dunedin, New Plymouth or Auckland.

Furthermore, to the career diplomat of the Foreign and Commonwealth Office, a posting to preside over the affairs of a tiny isolated community in the Caribbean or South Atlantic can scarcely be said to be the satisfying culmination of a brilliant career.

If they have come from that service they will be considerably less than high flyers. So there can be awesome appointment mistakes - as is suggested by a recent case of multiple arrogance in St. Helena - and, occasionally, yes occasionally, an inspired choice from outside and the prospect of maritally combined unstuffed success. And that, as you may have guessed, was the position in May 1991 when the people of St. Helena welcomed their new Governor and his wife.

Broadsheets of or about Caribbean dependent territories tend to play down the arrival and credentials of the latest new Governor - unless there is nothing less banal to highlight. Not so the *St. Helena News Review* of March 1991 whose banner headlines on page 1 read:

ALAN HOOLE IS NEW GOVERNOR
DELIA Returns As First Lady

My goodness, you may well think, a sort of Imelda Marcos is back to pick up the shoes she left behind. Not so. What follows is a kind of rare fairy tale of destiny or both - with the prospect, over time, of resounding success or dismal failure. How it is all handled will determine which it will be. But there seems little doubt. The omens are good. I know where to place my money.

You see, Alan Hoole had been in St. Helena before as Attorney General: 1978-1982 to be precise. He was married. His marriage folded. Released from one marital contract, Hoole entered in January 1982 into a second - with the daughter of Sgt. Smokey Clingham of the St. Helena Police and coxswain of the island lifeboat. Her name is Delia. A smitten Simon Winchester described her in the St. Helena section of his 1985 *Outposts* as 'a stunningly pretty Saint.' Elsewhere, in his piece on Anguilla, as 'a Saint of exquisite and serene beauty.'

There was more to it than that. Delia Clingham was one of a family of ten children, one being adopted, from the Longwood area of St. Helena. Christmas came one year and there were no presents for the children. Her mother told the disappointed children: 'Father Christmas didn't come because we must have forgotten to leave a light on, so I suppose he went past our house.' "That is the way she explained it to us," says Delia Hoole. "We might not have lots of money, she would say, but our family is the richest in love." And dignity too, I suspect.

Returning as the new Governor's wife to preside with her husband over the great occasions and the daily life of Plantation House was going to require careful and sensitive consideration, planning and performance. The bold decision was taken; but it could all go horribly wrong because the eyes and ears of every Saint would be watching ... watching, judging, and gossiping. As they say in the Caribbean 'You get you self up and de people knock you back down.' So the hard grind of the Turks and Caicos Islands and Anguilla was vital preparation for return to social eminence in St. Helena. Social eminence, but not social pretentiousness. That the Saints would not tolerate, as Delia well knew.

So she set about quietly being herself, seeking to achieve the ultimate popular accolade: 'Delia ain't change. She jus' da same.'

And in so doing she put herself on course for a caring supportive role in social work and concern for people. It began to be noticed when, at Christmas, Delia was spied, just as she used to be, walking in the crowds, having fun in the traditional St. Helenian way at that time of year. It was no coincidence that she conceived and organised in the grounds of Plantation House a Christmas fête to raise money for presents for the less fortunate, young and old, of St. Helena. She had not forgotten that present-less childhood Christmas of her own. At 16 and working, her first wages were £13 per month. She gave her mother £7 and kept six.

Plantation House was two hundred years old in November 1992. On leave with her husband in England during the summer of that year, Delia was already planning a special celebration with guests in eighteenth century-style costumes to mark the occasion.

Leadership style is all - or almost all - in small island communities. Machiavelli could have learned something from them. Alan Hoole and Delia certainly have. But for both the new Governor and his wife the occupation of Plantation House was not likely to be without potential problems.

"When we first discussed it after Alan had been offered the job," she says, "I was apprehensive as to how I would be received - whether

I would be accepted. I need not have worried, I suppose. We Saints are a warm people and I have been given tremendous support and encouragement from everyone since the day of our arrival. That has relaxed me. At times it has been hard work but very rewarding; and I don't think I could have coped without the help of all the people of St. Helena. I have been accepted from the beginning."

There was good reason. When Delia came up the landing steps of her native St. Helena as wife of the Governor, the first to greet and embrace her were her proud mother and father. She shook hands with the assembled officialdom, then walked through the crowds along by the sea wall with her parents, an arm around each shoulder. The symbolism was lost on none. The fact of it won over all, as she stood beside her husband for the swearing in ceremony that afternoon.

Nine months later, Delia Hoole recognised that for both her husband and herself the honeymoon period was over. What mattered now were achievements, not sentiments.

"My most rewarding experience so far," she said, "has been the formation of my ladies craft group which meets monthly at Plantation House. We are teaching each other and working together to raise money to benefit the less fortunate. I know that it is only a supportive rôle to Alan, but I think that its work will become increasingly important. At least, I hope so. Of course, the most significant problem facing us all and testing the loyalty of the Saints is our exclusion from the United Kingdom and the phased withdrawal of domestic work permits. It is a cause of deep frustration and anxiety. But we shall continue to fight it and we shall win, however long it takes."

These are not the conventional utterances of a conventional colonial wife in a British dependent island territory. But Alan Hoole is not a conventional governor either.

CHAPTER 10

The Governor

I called on Governor Hoole at his splendid office in The Castle as the public service generally began a reluctant return to work on 2nd January, 1992. We had not met before - apart that is from a brief conversation during the New Year's Day festivities at Francis Plain. He is slim, neat, direct and unstuffed; and, you soon discover, with the best lawyer's sharpness of intellect and nose for the heart of the matter. He is the sixtieth Governor of St. Helena, twenty-eighth under the Crown.

"The production standards in The Castle," he says "are high compared with other similar places in the Caribbean. I keep telling them this; but I don't think they believe me because they have nothing to compare themselves with. Look at the work put out by our Printing Office." He handed me a bound volume of the *Laws of St. Helena for 1990.* "Legislation in some Caribbean countries is an unconsolidated mess. So it can be difficult, even for lawyers, to know precisely what the law is. Here I have each year's legislation bound and on my desk within days after the start of the new year. That's really something. And the official Gazette is a model of printing style and layout, just right for St. Helena. None of the cyclostyled stuff you get elsewhere in places you and I know."

The Governor's office and the adjoining Executive Council Chamber are colonial anachronisms alive and well, matched only in cultured seclusion and elegance by those of Gibraltar. There are shelves with leather-bound books of great age; and framed photographs of former Governors round the dark walls. There was, until a recent unlamented Governor blocked it up, even a small spyhole in the great doors to the office so that staff could see without disturbing him whether the moment was appropriate for gentle knocking and request for permission to enter into the Governor's presence.

I asked a relatively senior Saint in the Civil Service about that earlier regime.

"He was just a pig. Nothin' else to say. We called him so." I thought it best to leave it at that.

Governor Hoole has refreshingly original ideas. I had brought him a list of fifty water colours and coloured engravings of late eighteenth and early nineteenth century St. Helena which had formed a bequest to the Royal Commonwealth Society Library in London. The unique historic contents of that fine library appeared to be about to be dispersed.

"I have put in a bid for them if the library is closed."

"I know," I said. "The Librarian was delighted to receive your gubernatorial telephone call from the middle of the South Atlantic. I don't think she has fully recovered from the surprise of it."

"I want to get some fine old art work to liven up these walls and perhaps also those of Plantation House, although it is a bit damp there. We are opening up the House so that ordinary people can begin to feel that it belongs to them, and they to it. We had a group of senior school children in the other day. Went very well, I think. And as you know we had the New Year's Eve dance in this office and the Executive Council room. With the dividing doors wide open, it was just about big enough. When I came in this morning, it was cleaned and tidied so beautifully you would never know what had been going on here. All my books and papers were back exactly as they were beforehand. The women of the Girl Guides Association did it all, including the splendid floral decorations ... You will want to meet the Legislative Council members of course. You know them all, I expect. The Council now has a Speaker. The Governor no longer presides."

He handed me a copy of the Constitution. "Have a look at the Governor's special responsibilities. You will find something interesting."

There they were, the usual subjects: the public service, defence, external affairs, internal security and the police, the administration of justice, finance. And - shipping.

"I've not known that anywhere else," he said. "It obviously reflects the importance attached in London to the shipping link and to the rôle of the *RMS* itself, as the lifeblood of the community."

If a departing Hong Kong is omitted from the list, there are ten populated British colonies still surviving: Anguilla, Bermuda, The British Virgin Islands, Cayman Islands, The Falklands, Gibraltar, Montserrat, Pitcairn, Turks and Caicos Islands - and St. Helena. Tiny Pitcairn apart, they all have an advanced form of self-government although there are differences between them in this respect. Turks and Caicos have recently climbed out of annual grant-in-aid from London. The Falklands and Anguilla too. Only St. Helena remains on the subsidy list. Pitcairn is the only one without a resident governor. In the past, the Governor of colonial Fiji was also Governor of Pitcairn. Now it is the British High Commissioner in Wellington, New Zealand, the day to day administration of Pitcairn affairs being located in Auckland.

As in the case of all other colonies, the executive authority of St. Helena and its Dependencies is vested in the sovereign and exercised by the Governor on Her Majesty's behalf, either directly or through officers subordinate to him. The 1988 St. Helena Constitution Order differs in a number of ways from its 1966 predecessor. The present Order has seven more sections, 56 instead of 49. There are some significant changes in wording and content, not least the inclusion of the Governor's special responsibilities (a better phrase for what used to be described as reserved subjects); and the expansion of the circumstances under which the Governor is not obliged to consult his Executive Council or to accept their advice when he has. One interesting new exclusion is 'any matter concerning the exercise of the executive authority of the Dependencies.' This clearly establishes that the Executive Councillors of St. Helena have no policy-making rôle or function in respect of Tristan da Cunha or Ascension.

The law-making powers reflect a similar distinction. Section 27 of the Constitution says:

'Subject to the provisions of the Constitution -

(a)   the Governor with the advice and consent of the Legislative Council may make laws for the peace, order and good government of St. Helena;

(b) the Governor in his discretion may make laws for the peace, order and good government of Ascension and Tristan da Cunha, respectively.'

No doubt, in practice, the respective Administrators will be consulted by a Governor of St. Helena beforehand; and will themselves initiate proposals for new or amending legislation.

There is one little known but essential document which determines the 'pecking order' at official and social functions in British Colonial territories.   It roughly reflects British metropolitan practice in respect of the Crown, the Cabinet, Parliament, the Judiciary, the Established Church, the Diplomatic Corps - Commonwealth High Commissioners and non-Commonwealth Ambassadors - and the Civil Service. It is called a Table of Precedence. Here is the one for St. Helena:

TABLE OF PRECEDENCE

ST. HELENA

1. The Governor [or Officer Administering the Government]
2. The Bishop of St. Helena
3. The Chief Justice of St. Helena
4. The Speaker
5. Ex-Officio Members of Executive Council -
    (a) Chief Secretary
    (b) Financial Secretary
    (c) Attorney General
6. Unofficial Members of Executive Council (according to date of first appointment)
7. The Judges of the Court of Appeal -

    (a) President
    (b) Members (according to date of first appointment)
8. Elected Members of Legislative Council (according to date of first appointment)
9. The Administrator of -
    (a) Ascension
    (b) Tristan da Cunha
10. Members of the Consular Corps
11. The Sheriff of St. Helena
12. Heads of Departments
13. Justices of the Peace
14. Chairmen of Statutory Corporations

This is clearly a list which has been specially tailored for the circumstances of St. Helena. And so it should be. It is different in those other British territories where there are Chief Minister, local ministerial responsibility for finance and other subjects, no resident Bishop, no Chief Justice as such and varying *ex officio* membership of the Executive and Legislative Councils.

The fact that a Table of Precedence has been determined and made known does not, however, mean that all argument is stilled about who comes where. Far from it - notably among the wives of contract expatriates who seem to become, with notable exceptions, obsessed, miserable and carping about where they sit and whom they sit next to. I have known an expatriate judge's wife develop in my office a high performance rating in hysterics because she was to be presented to the Queen after the locally born wife of the Minister of Finance whom she detested. The fact that, rightly or wrongly, the Table of Precedence for the country said so, mattered not a jot. Contented morning coffee consumption was impossible, since the antipathy was mutual.

The lady concerned got herself into such a state of frenzy at the presentation rehearsal that assault and battery in white gloves and hat was barely prevented by assembled officialdom. Her husband's eccentricities included the habit of disappearing off the bench to the club across the road in the middle of a case and forgetting to come back. Part of the reason seemed clear.

So what then, as we approach the twenty-first century, is the British colonial island governor of today? In spite of his responsibilities, he certainly cannot see himself as an autocrat in any aspect of the business of government. Nor is he - thankfully say some, regretfully say others - an oracular dispenser of wisdom, administrative judgement and vision. He has to be a catalyst, the manager and manipulator of a team, a patient listener and a skilled chairman. His success will be measured by those over whose lives he presides in terms of trust and confidence in his style, empathy, impartiality, personality and energy.

There was one governor in the Caribbean who walked around all day - and sometimes at night - with a copy of the island Constitution in his pocket. Whenever he was in doubt, he would pull it out for instant consultation. Result: the more he consulted it, the more he needed to - as the rows and confrontations with a frustrated Chief Minister grew more frequent and more audible.

The basic but most elusive skill is flexibility without weakness. Try it: the boundaries are close. Another perhaps is a decision-making capacity without the presumption of infallibility. Social graces without condescension are fundamental; but not so easy to sustain without the danger of alcoholic disintegration in response to the cumulative affect of claustrophobic - and in some instances stultifying - social insularity. And there is the important question of a balanced relationship with colleagues, both fellow expatriates and locals in the civil service, all of whom are also subordinates.

There is a loneliness to be borne with patience and an essential element of aloofness without stand-offishness, warmth without over-chumminess. Whatever an island governor does, wherever he goes, to whose house and when and what for and who with, are matters under the constant scrutiny of perceptive local eyes - watching, judging, gossiping and reacting. This is where Alan Hoole is so singularly fortunate. His wife is his informal eyes and ears of St.

Helena, an invaluable partner and interpretative aid to popular sentiment and thinking. Pillow talk can be constructive in the right people.

Leadership qualities? Of course. A *sine qua non* you would say for a contemporary colonial island governor. But what middle-grade diplomatic officer has been grounded in the business of managing a government, however small. It is a bit like being trained to sit in someone else's shop and to report what is going on in it. Then having to go and run your own without the authority normally vested in a chief executive. For a chief executive is what the colonial governor of today certainly is not. And should he have *folies de grandeur* that he is, then assuredly he is in the wrong job and will come unstuck. As Henry Kissinger said 'Power is the ultimate aphrodisiac.' And a recipe for downfall in a democratic island society by any who would seek to exercise it.

> 'What is needed is a wise, sympathetic and patient man, endowed with a sense of humour, not over-sensitive about his dignity, and content to gain his point by persuasion rather than pressure. Such a one will be able to do as he pleases with the people; a pompous or choleric person will have the island about his ears before he has been there a month.'

The island was not St. Helena. The ocean was not the South Atlantic. It was the tiny island of Niue, population 5000, in the South Pacific. The words are those of Basil Thomson who wrote them in 1902. But they do not seem far off the mark nearly a century later.

CHAPTER 11

Justice

The Courthouse of St. Helena is white painted with blue facings but it does not advertise its presence. One reason may be that it is conveniently next to the Police Station. Indeed both, together on the other side with the Public Library, are in one connected building, past the entrance to the Castle in the Grand (and welcoming) Square of Jamestown.

There is no sign to indicate what may, when the court is sitting, be going on inside. This may be because everyone knows what is. So it doesn't need to announce itself. Or it may be because it doubles as the Legislative Council Chamber when the seating is rearranged and all evidence of its other life is removed. It is perhaps the closest circumstance - not unique to St. Helena - in which the functions of the legislative and the judicial arms of government come, so to speak, to meet.

Two eighteen pounder black-painted cast iron howitzers flank the entrance to the Court House, their wheels embedded in the pavement. If you look closely, you can read on one side the name of the manufacturer:

John Sturges and Co
Bowling
Yorkshire.

There is no indication of the year of manufacture.

Paying his last official visit to the island was the Chief Justice of St. Helena and its dependencies since 1983 - Sir John Farley Spry. And at 82, spry he was. From the same year he had also been President of the Gibraltar Court of Appeal. All this after a distinguished legal career, mainly in colonial East Africa. But after starting in Uganda, he went in 1944 - as I did in 1946 - to Palestine for the ebbing years of the British mandate, he in Jerusalem and I in Gaza. He left on the last RAF plane before the birth of the State of Israel on 15th May, 1948. His one declared innocent hobby is conchology.

Sir John and his wife, Stella, had come to St. Helena by the *RMS* for the January 1992 session of the Supreme Court. "One unusual feature of the administration of justice in St. Helena," he told me "is that in the lower court the Attorney General advises the magistrates, the prosecution and the defence. This is because there are no lawyers in private practice on the island." An indication, it would seem, of the law-abiding quality and character of the community.

"Since about 1985, St. Helena has enjoyed one very interesting procedural provision. An accused, if committed in the lower court, has the option of being tried by the judge alone or by the judge with a jury of eight. Since everyone on St. Helena is related to almost everyone else in one way or another, this avoids the difficulty of not being able to find a totally 'impartial' jury. It has worked very well. In maybe a dozen such instances since 1985, in all but one case, the accused has opted to be tried by judge alone."

I thought about this for the British Virgin Islands. There it is almost impossible to get a jury conviction of a 'native', even in serious drug and drug-related offenses. The result is that the bevy of lawyers who constitute the local Bar Association make rich pickings, their fees paid, of course, from the proceeds of drug dealing by a discharged but perhaps far from innocent defendant. As Lord Hailsham once said on a BBC TV programme

'In the English system (of justice), it is fundamental that a verdict of not guilty does not mean that the accused did not commit the crime with which he was charged. Merely that it was not proven beyond reasonable doubt.'

In my early days in the British Virgin Islands, I saw a blatant piece of reckless driving and collision on a road not far from the main police station. A sergeant arrived, questioned the two drivers and prepared to depart.

"You are going to charge the driver of the offending car I presume?" I said.

"Oh no," he replied "but I wahn (warn) him."

"But surely, grossly negligent driving. I saw it all and will give evidence, if necessary. Open and shut case I would have thought."

He demurred.

"Well why ever not?"

He looked at me. "We can't prosecute he. He bahn (born) here." A new angle on the concept of estoppel perhaps.

I was walking downhill from The Briars to Jamestown. Easy, they had said, only about a mile. Except that the descent ratio is fearsome for aging leg muscles. To the right and up into the sky, the sheer stark cliff rocks, brown and broken and serried and unrelieved by any vegetation. To the left, plunging down into the abyss below, the flax and prickly pear-studded bottom half. The narrow winding road carved its way, clinging to the edge of eternity. For protection, a low but solid stone wall. Looking over it gave me close acquaintance with vertigo. Especially when I saw how deep the retaining wall was that kept the road together.

I sought refuge against the craggy cliff wall as I padded down, complying with the normal practice of facing on-coming motor traffic. Not that there was much. The St. Helena road code is that vehicles going down Ladder Hill Road or Side Path into Jamestown give way at the passing bays to those on the way up. So walking round a blind right hand corner should be OK, it seemed. I could not be in the way of two passing cars.

A police van was coming up. It stopped opposite me. An Inspector with a flourishing moustache leaned out.

"Excuse me, sir. It is the practice in St. Helena to walk downhill on the left next to the outside wall. I wouldn't want you to be crushed against that nasty cliff, would I?"

"No. I suppose not. I'll do as you say. Of course. Without looking down. Thank you."

"Thank you sir, and have a good evening."

Now that I thought, is an example of admirable police public relations with an ignorant visitor. Courtesy Cop. An idea to be copied - from St. Helena?

On 30th October, 1992, the name of the successor to Sir John Spry as Chief Justice of St. Helena was announced from The Castle. He is Geoffrey William Martin, Chief Justice of the Kingdom of Tonga from 1986 - 1990. I cannot but think that St. Helena will prove to be judicially refreshing after the labyrinthine litigiousness of that part of South Pacific Polynesia.

CHAPTER 12

Eric

Eric Benjamin is 59 and a man of parts. You are likely to find him in many rôles and in many guises. I sought him out on New Year's Eve in Jamestown at a charity dance open to the public in the local community centre. It was 10 p.m. Too early it seemed, since there was but one solitary couple in the centre of the floor.

On the bandstand, a small group of musicians played both a foxtrot and the waiting game, before the invasion that would soon come. The leader had his ear down listening to the tuning of his electronic piano.

"Eric," I said. "How splendid to see you again, especially on such an evening." The Gettogethers Orchestra was making ready for a long night.

On Sunday afternoon, I found him again. He was in overalls, pumping up the rear tyre of his motor car outside his London Gift Shop. It is modest in size and appearance even by English village standards. Next to it is a door at street level which opens to a narrow staircase with a head-trap for tall visitors. There are two intriguing rooms above. One contains an array of the musical instruments which a Salvation Army-trained Eric Benjamin plays. The other in his inner sanctum, his office, his reception room for visitors, his study, his modest escape from pursuit. For Eric Benjamin is nothing if not, in St. Helena, someone for everyone. Until the 1993 General Election he was the senior elected member of the Legislative Council, a member of Executive Council and Chairman of the Public Works and Services Committee. He had represented St. Paul's constituency since 1970.

On Monday morning, I sat in the public gallery of the pro tem Courthouse for the first cases to be heard before the visiting Chief Justice. Eric was there. He was clad in a black gown, the attire of a lay advocate. He appeared for the accused in two cases of unlawful carnal knowledge of girls below the age of consent. His pleading in the first case may well have resulted in a more leniently humane outcome than I had thought likely at the beginning.

"There have been so many changes in St. Helena," said Eric, when I saw him later that day in the inner sanctum. "But in general the Saints' standards and quality of life is being preserved. In some respects even improved: the education system in particular, although we still have a shortage of good teachers and their salaries are pitiful. Family life has become easier and social tensions have lessened as a result of our house building programme. It is now rare to find three generations living in the one house. The energies of the young are going into housing which is now affordable for many and that is great. Middle management skills are still lacking. Drinking remains the worst social problem, but it is not as bad as it was. There is the occasional drunken brawl, but no knives or similar weapons."

"We still need a bank. We have managed so far to survive without one, so I suppose we could go on doing so. But we badly need a lending institution sympathetic to the needs of the people and for every day commercial transactions. At present everything is paid for in cash. There are no credit facilities and only limited investment loans from public funds. That seriously handicaps private initiative and development."

"Then there is the new ship. We Saints are proud of it but we in St. Helena must always have control over that. There have been great developments in water and electricity; and sea wall protection is being improved. All very satisfactory."

"Yet ... " He looked reflective. "There is one serious unresolved problem. You know what that is - the matter of citizenship and entry into the United Kingdom. It is not a matter of the Saints wanting to troop off to England *en masse*. It is a question of status and above all, dignity. We are deprived of dignity by the present exclusion. We won't accept it. We will keep on trying until we win. We must do so and Britain must listen in the end."

I hope he is right. He should be.

In dependent territory public life - and, for that matter, also in independent Commonwealth countries - there are numerous examples of elected politicians who are former civil servants. When elections are imminent and electioneering begins in the Caribbean, it is well nigh impossible in practice to ensure that senior civil servants stay aloof from and uninvolved in party platform activity. Whose country is it anyway, they will argue as you wrestle with drafting the latest circular instructions about what they can do and supposedly not do as election fever runs high.

Then, of course, there are the permanent secretaries and others who see entry into political life as a natural next step in personal career enhancement. So they get leave of absence, throw their hats into the electoral ring and get on with street-corner oratory and intrigue. If they succeed, they resign from the civil service and take their seats in parliament. If they fail, they lick their wounds and are permitted to take on again where, temporarily, they left off. In neither case is any loss of income faced. Indeed those who are politically successful can mostly look forward not only to career enhancement but to bank balance boosts as well. There is no nonsense about ministers not being paid more than senior civil servants.

Not so in St. Helena. Saints elected to the Legislative Council receive only daily attendance and travel allowances. No annual stipend or pension. This disincentive in respect of the democratic process would seem to be crippling; and likely to throw up candidates for election of either those few with private incomes and endless leisure or the perennially jobless.

The St. Helena solution may be unique. It must be the only Commonwealth country where you can be an elected politician and a civil servant at the same time. And receive money from public funds in respect of both.

Cathy Hopkins is a music teacher at Prince Andrew School. Her main instrument is the clarinet and her musical interests are mainstream

Mozart and Haydn. She is English and first came to St. Helena as a VSO. Her husband Keith is a Saint and also a teacher of carpentry, after many years in the Public Works Department. Cathy is tall with a strong personality and a sense of humour, as I was to discover.

She had been to England and was travelling back to St. Helena on the *RMS* with her husband. For her, like Eric Benjamin and her other fellow Legislative Councillors in 1992, the main resentments of the Saints lay in British Government continued refusal to grant equality of status and right of entry into Britain; together with the announced withdrawal of work permits for domestic employment from 1994. I asked her about the Prince Andrew School hall.

"It is used for a variety of school and community purposes and is a valuable acquisition accordingly. But the stage is badly designed, the sound is terrible and the flat concrete floor means that no one except those in the front few rows can see what is going on on the stage. The sight lines are impossible ..."

Cathy talked to me again briefly at the Plantation House reception the night before the *RMS* sailed north for Tenerife on Thursday, 6th February.

"You have been writing, I hear," she said.

"Yes."

"What about?"

"Not about Napoleon."

"Praise be for that. I am sick and tired of books about St. Helena and Napoleon. Do you know what I've always wanted to do?"

"Tell me."

"One Bastille Day, I would love to go up to Longwood and paint a big sign and nail it on a tree. Do you know what I would put on that sign?"

"No."

"I would put on it:

'THE DUKE OF WELLINGTON SLEPT HERE.'"

Now this, I thought, is a woman of spirit. She would no doubt accompany her notice with some swooning upper register clarinet shrieks from the Berlioz Symphonie Fantastique.

THE BRIARS PAVILION
(Home to Napoleon from October to December 1815)

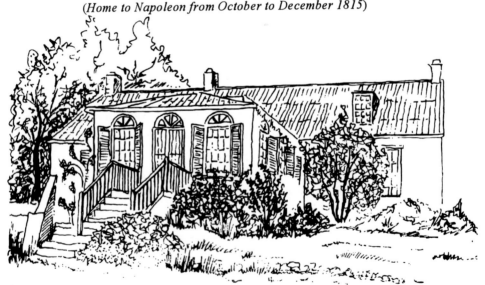

THE HOUSE OF COUNT BERTRAND
(Grand Marshal of the Palace)

CHAPTER 13

The City

If you have not been to St. Helena, you may not be able to imagine Half Tree Hollow: 'The City' says Second Engineer Myron Benjamin, who lives there and is proud of it. There is neither a half tree nor a hollow. No one seems to know how the name came about. The land is a far from gently sloping escarpment on which, apparently higgledy-piggledy, are scores of houses, school, community centre, and church. Jehovah's Witnesses are following fast with a hall on a prime site. All this would be nothing if it were not laid out before the vast panorama of the South Atlantic Ocean. All 180° of it, a thousand feet below, a vast limitless oleaginous swell.

There are countries where the cost of such sites beggar the imagination. Such splendour is taken for granted at Half Tree Hollow. Hardly noticed in fact. More important is water and sewage leaking from one septic tank to the site below. Dust, lack of natural shelter and of landscaping gives it all a starkness that is real. It was a sort of unplanned betrayal, I suppose. At least initially; because now efforts are being made to encourage flowers and vegetables from this unpromising wilderness. To face daily 'commuting' down the Ladder Hill Road and back in the evening may seem less than enchanting. But not to those who live there. They take it for granted: like the harsh brown rock on which they build, the bushes of prickly pear and the occasional eucalyptus tree.

Anyhow, the residents are at the centre of the world stage. As the road begins up the slope, there is a great sign:

COMMONWEALTH AVENUE.

But that is not all. Half Tree Hollow has its own amateur radio station from which an island ham operator does indeed talk to the world. And he receives verification cards, sometimes with a mini-mum of apparently inexplicable symbols as the address. This example from across the world is a tribute, I thought, to the distribution genius and imagination of oft-maligned post offices and postal staff. Here is how the DX-er's card was addressed:

ZD7DP
HTH
SHI
SAO

Nothing else. And yet the card was delivered to the correct destination. I asked for an explanation. This what I was told:

ZD7DP is the call sign of the station

HTH is - yes it is - Half Tree Hollow

SHI is, of course, St. Helena Island

SAO is South Atlantic Ocean.

Simple - once you know. But how did the post offices which handled this singular piece of mail?

The relative economic buoyancy of St. Helena and the notable differences since a decade ago are due to employment opportunities which have existed on Ascension for a sustained period and those which have emerged in the Falklands since the war and are a direct consequence of it. It is indeed an ill wind..

The Employment Unit of the Employment and Social Services Department handles the recruitment of Saints for both destinations and monitors what happens to them there. On 3rd January, 1992, with her office just recovering from the New Year holiday exhaustions, Sylvia Buckley allowed me, unannounced, to ply her with questions. At the end of November, 1991, she told me, there were 249 Saints - 139 males and 110 females - working under contract in The Falklands. All were unaccompanied by dependent families and the majority were domestic assistants working for an international catering concession company. They were paid £487.50 per month tax free for a sixty hour working week. They were housed in single unit accommodation in barracks. Meals were provided.

The NAAFI employed 37 Saints earning £2.10 per hour as

cleaners and general snackbar and club assistants. They worked a 48 hour week and earned about £400 per month. A construction company had 39 Saints on their payroll as clerks, carpenters, masons and general semi-skilled workers. They earned £560 per month for a 63 hour week and received a bonus of £650 at the end of the year.

The Falkland Islands Government employed clerks, hospital nurses, electricians, power house operators and mechanics on a part tax-free and part taxable basis. No wonder Prince Andrew School placed such emphasis on courses in technical trades.

The Falkland Islands Company had one female clerk from St. Helena. She earned about £800 per month. The Property Services Agency employed 43 Saints - 32 male and 11 female - as drivers, cooks and labourers. They lived in tough conditions in portacabins working on rural road construction; but, with overtime, they earned about £1,000 per month.

All this is way beyond what can be earned on St. Helena itself where an average basic wage is around £40 per week. The sacrifices become understandable and, in retrospect at least, worth enduring for most. The new house construction in Half Tree Hollow; the microwaves; the washing machines; the Hi-Fis and above all, the videos, are the result. Plus something approaching parking problems - cars, not donkeys - when the *RMS* lies off Jamestown.

On Ascension there is a similar story - 475 Saints at the end of November, 1991 on employment contracts. There are ten separate employing companies, including the BBC. Of a total population of 1,067 on Ascension in June, 1991, over 50% were Saints.

Summed up, 850 Saints were working in the Falklands and Ascension from a total St. Helena population of about 5,500. And that is about a third of the available work force - a brain drain, or rather a skill drain indeed. If you add the Saints who are officers and crew of the *RMS St. Helena,* and the 110 Saints on the disappearing domestic work permits in Britain, you have well over 1,000 individual Saints employed outside the island of their birth. Include their dependants or families and you touch the greater part of the population.

This is why the *RMS St. Helena* was currently undertaking two shuttle services - St. Helena-Ascension-St. Helena - to take workers to and from Ascension both for that island and for connection with the once-weekly RAF return flight through Ascension to the Falklands. And why I was glad to be wrong, as things turned out, in predicting in 1986 a degree of social unrest because of unemployment.

Add to that the published statistics about motor vehicles: at the end of 1960 there were 282. In January 1992, 2,203. May the bubble of Ascension and The Falklands not burst, say the wise heads. The consequences for the Saints could be dire.

St. Helena has no natural resources and no exports of significance. Any enterprise which seeks to redress that imbalance, however modestly, deserves to be noticed. Hence the St. Helena Canning Company. Its manager/operator/owner was a passenger on Voyage 6 South. And not for the first time. Douglas Wallace, a Mancunian of Scottish origin, travelled twenty-six times on the old *RMS* and by early 1992 five times on the new. He has been a resident of St. Helena for fourteen years and is married to a Saint.

He was back home in St. Helena in time for the start of the January to June tuna season, after a marketing visit to Britain and to Switzerland where his financial backers are. The company is registered under the International Business Companies legislation which was enacted in the British Virgin Islands in 1984 and which has been copied elsewhere in the Caribbean since then.

From the same year, Douglas Wallace has been using what he calls the 'salmon process' and not the usual tuna process. This gives a slightly different texture and taste from the standard product. To achieve this he does two things: he uses fresh, not frozen, fish almost exclusively; and he processes and cooks at the same time instead of pre-cooking and then processing. And there is tight quality control. Effective, I thought, on my one brief tasting session.

In the skipjack season, the company would reckon on taking in a ton and a quarter of fish a day, working from 7 a.m. to 9 p.m. And that is tuna caught by individual fishermen only three or four miles out from Rupert's Bay. They also can albacore, a white meat tuna, and yellow fin.

The production target for 1992 was 200,000 170 gramme tins. The first of them were to go on the shelves of a British supermarket chain in February, 1992: a St. Helena South Atlantic first to put beside, if not yet to match in quantity and gourmet appeal, the crayfish tails of Tristan da Cunha.

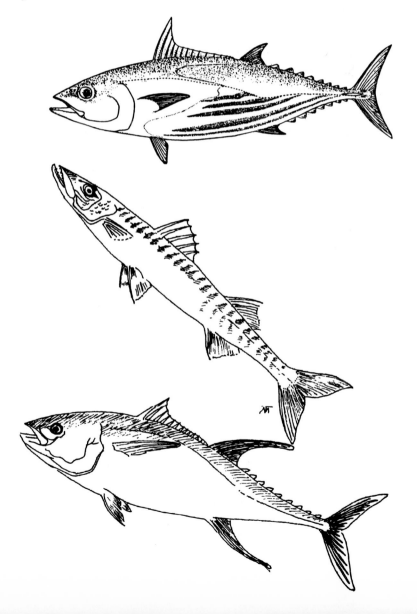

CHAPTER 14

Notices

When I was a regular attender at Presbyterian church services, the one break in the religious proceedings came when an Elder of the Kirk would come before the congregation and say: "Here are the notices for the coming week."

We would then hear about a forthcoming meeting of the Ladies Guild, the Sunday School picnic or a call for volunteers to help paint the church hall. It was often the notices that told more about the life and activities of the church than the service or sermon.

Public notices or signs of one kind or another reveal as much about a community as anything else. When you study - really notice - notices, they begin to tell you more than perhaps you initially realised.

On the external wall to the left of the Castle entrance are these:

I JOHN DVTTON
GOVERNOVR OF THIS ISLE
FIRST ERECTED THIS FORTIFICA
TION FOR THE ENGLISH EAST INDIA
COMPA IVNE Ye 4 AN DOM 1659
OPERA TESTANTVRDEME

And below it on the same wall is this tablet:

THE ABOVE STONE ALLUDES
TO A
FORT BUILT IN 1659, TAKEN DOWN
AND
THE PRESENT CASTLE BUILT
BY GOVERNOR ROBERTS IN 1708;

THE HON'BLE BRIGDr DALLAS,
THE LAST GOVERNOR
OF THE
HON'BLE UNITED EAST INDIA COMPANY
IN CLEARING AWAY FOUND IT UPSIDE DOWN IN PART
OF THE FOUNDATION OF THE CASTLE AND RESTORED IT
AS NOW PLACED
AD. 1834.

On the left entrance arch above a polished mounted gun

IN COMMEMORATION OF
THE THREE HUNDREDTH ANNIVERSARY OF
CAPTAIN JOHN DUTTON'S
LANDING ON THE 5TH MAY 1659
FROM WHICH TIME ST. HELENA
HAS BEEN A BRITISH POSSESSION

1659   1959

The roads of St. Helena are dauntingly narrow, winding and hazardous for those unfamiliar with them. They twist and turn upon themselves and cling precariously to hillsides and rock faces. Way up in the mist-afflicted 'highlands' is St. Paul's Church. Nearby, two typical St. Helenian roads meet. A sign says without a blush:

HALT
MAJOR ROAD AHEAD.

Near Plantation House is this unexpected notice:

THE AGRICULTURE AND NATURAL RESOURCES
DEPARTMENT SCOTLAND

Further on you will see another sign with a pointing arrow which says just this:

THE TOMB

You walk down a long meandering path through the bush clad silence of the hills to a clearing. In the centre there is indeed what looks to be a tomb surrounded by iron railings. There is a sentry box and a slot for a visitors' book. But neither sentry nor visitors' book; and no notice plaque or stone to indicate that it was to this place that the body of Napoleon Bonaparte was brought by his retinue upon his death on 5th May, 1821. You might think that this sort of arrogant anonymity is a bit like that of the postage stamps of Britain, the only country not to have its name on them. In fact, it was because the British and French authorities could not agree as to how Napoleon was to be described - General or Emperor.

... On 7th September, 1840, Dumont d'Urville's *Astrolabe* was seen to drop anchor at James Bay along with Captain Jacquinot's *Zelee*. They were returning from a voyage of exploration in the Antarctic.

Appendix III shows the letter in facsimile written on board the *Astrolabe* on 9th September, 1840 and published in *The Times* of London on 2nd December that year, together with a print of the relevant extract.

On 8th October, 1840, a frigate *La Belle Poule* and a corvette *La Favorite* arrived for the repatriation of Napoleon's body. They had set out from France in July ..

* * *

A notable feature of contemporary Jamestown and indeed the whole island of St. Helena is its cleanliness: the result of an effective government and community campaign. There are 'trash bins' at strategic points all over Jamestown. Obviously, they are used.

Virtually the only 'rubbish' I saw was dead leaves; and these were quickly swept up and removed. There are modern garbage collection vehicles which, like the great hearse, negotiate the roads with difficulty. Standard British black plastic bags dot the countryside. As the full ones are picked up and thrown into the back grinder, an empty replacement bag goes into the bushes for the next consignment. Many of the rubbish men on the trucks are not men at all - but clean overall-clad women. CHUCK 'N CHEW urges the big sign on the front of the garbage truck. They obviously do; and it does.

There is a splendid freshwater public swimming pool just below The Castle in Jamestown. The notice describes it as:

PROJECT BONAPARTE

on the site of a tennis court built by the Royal Engineers in 1889 and opened by Governor G.C. Guy in November, 1979.

Nearby is another notice of a slightly different kind:

Anyone having anything
to eat or drink or smoke
is asked to
please use the
MULE YARD area.

There is no indication as to where this sanctuary is. You are expected to know and to go there. Unless, like the mule, you are 'an offspring of a mare by a he-ass used as a beast of draught and burden and noted for obstinacy' and thus, like me, fail to find out.

A short distance away in the garden near Ann's Place, there is a marble column set in stone with the lengthy inscription shown overleaf.

THIS COLUMN
WAS ERECTED BY THE
COMMANDER, OFFICERS AND CREW
OF HER MAJESTY'S BRIG
WATERWITCH
TO THE MEMORY OF THEIR SHIPMATES
WHO DIED WHILE SERVING ON
THE COAST OF AFRICA
A.D. 1839-1843
THE GREATER NUMBER DIED
WHILE ABSENT IN CAPTURED SLAVE VESSELS.
THEIR REMAINS WERE
EITHER LEFT IN DIFFERENT PARTS OF AFRICA
OR GIVEN TO THE SEA
THEIR GRAVES ALIKE UNDISTINGUISHED.
THIS ISLAND
IS SELECTED FOR THE RECORD
BECAUSE THREE LIE BURIED HERE
AND BECAUSE THE DECEASED AS WELL AS
THEIR SURVIVING COMRADES
EVER MET THE WARMEST WELCOME FROM
ITS INHABITANTS

4th JULY 1843

And so it is to this day when a stranger arrives in St. Helena. On the side of the deep retaining wall, half way up Ladder Hill Road, a white painted greeting from 1984 was still there in 1992:

WELCOME PRINCE ANDREW

Facing out to sea from above what seems to be two great holes in the cliffs; but which constitutes all that outwardly is left of former defence barracks, is

WELCOME RMS ST. HELENA
FAREWELL RMS ST. HELENA ISLAND

The old ship had been renamed *St. Helena Island* to distinguish it from the new *RMS* then under construction.

Halls, buildings and shops in Jamestown all have their notices, although the impeccably clean Wellington House - otherwise known as Yon's Café - shelters shyly under the cloak of anonymity. It has no sign at all to tell you what it is. The churches are not so reticent, not least the Kingdom Hall of Jehovah's Witnesses. Then there is the Queen Mary Theatre, but you find on entrance that it is now a grocery store. There is a Freemason's Hall and perhaps the most intriguing notice of all:

COURT OF ST. JAMES
ANCIENT ORDER OF FORESTERS
NO. 5635
ESTABLISHED 1871

Match these warm St. Helenian notices with one of a quite different kind in Simonstown, the South African naval base an hour or so by train from Cape Town. In front of a modest three storey white building facing the ocean and backing on to the cliffside is a pair of large notices. The white one has this in black lettered English and Afrikaans:

S.A. NAVAL HEADQUARTERS
DIRECTORATE NAVAL ACCOUNTS

To the left of this is a big yellow notice with black lettering in three languages. It reads:

WARNING
ACCESS PROHIBITED
Any person entering this area
without proper authority
does so at his peril

By order of the
Minister of Defence

Goodness me. Might have the vote book thrown at him, I suppose.
Or last year's auditor's report.

MEMORIAL STONE
South Atlantic Post Office of 1645

I - *RMS ST. HELENA* WORKS HER CARGO AT ANCHOR OFF JAMESTOWN

II - DOWNTOWN JAMESTOWN FROM HALF WAY UP JACOB'S LADDER

III - Under the shade away from the mid-day sun

IV - JACOB'S LADDER - 699 STEPS UP FROM JAMESTOWN

V - PLANTATION HOUSE

VI - DELIA, MRS. ALAN HOOLE AT PLANTATION HOUSE

VII - The Post Office

VIII - FLAGSTAFF AND THE BARN

IX - SANDY BAY FROM MOUNT PLEASANT

X - Gateway to the Castle

XI - Fishing with rod and line

CHAPTER 15

The Fax of Life

The road up the eastern rock face out of Jamestown is called Side Path. It climbs steadily if precariously to Button Up Corner and Two Gun Saddle, passes the Judge's Lodge at Seaview, on past The Devil's Punch Bowl to Napoleon's Longwood House. Below Seaview, there is a deep luxuriant valley with the massive High Knoll Fort and the Heart Shape Waterfall above and to the west.

In the valley is a house called The Briars; and it was there that Napoleon Bonaparte stayed for the first two months of his exile on St. Helena. Today, The Briars is probably the first point of call for visitors taking a day circuit of the island in Cecil Corker's charabanc. Some may not notice - or if they do, will not have time to investigate - the electronic and communications marvels that are housed in an assembly of neatly sited and maintained buildings close by. They can hardly miss the great shining disc pointing into the sky and confirming that The Briars is also the St. Helena headquarters of Cable and Wireless - The World Telephone Company - as the first page of the modest yellow-covered St. Helena telephone directory for 1991 proudly proclaims.

It is not without justification. And it is undeniable that the past three years have seen such dramatic developments in the nature and quality of telecommunications within and without St. Helena as to cause the Cable and Wireless operation to stand with that of the *RMS* and the shipping link in importance for government, business and family life on the island. Instant direct international telephone dialling and that great modern invention, the facsimile machine, have revolutionised life on St. Helena and transformed the meaning of island isolation in a shrinking world.

For Cable and Wireless on St. Helena, it all began in 1899 when the company, wholly owned by the British Government and barely twenty years old, took over the Eastern Telegraph Company and established a base in Rupert's Valley. This was a regeneration station installed to support the submarine cables which had suddenly become of front-line importance with the outbreak of the Boer War in South Africa in the same year.

In the early years of the new century, the station was transferred to The Briars and introduced a telegram service for the island. Ship to shore operations were begun in 1940. When cables were abandoned in 1969, the St. Helena station shrank into insignificance and apparently irreversible decline. The island was at the end of a path which led to nowhere, its status historic and sentimental and uneconomic.

Apart from the introduction of a telex service in 1978, that remained the situation when George Stevens became General Manager in an all-Saint operation in 1979: one which was rapidly becoming a quaint anachronism and one for which no one in the London headquarters of Cable and Wireless could see an economically viable solution. It remained on the world 'rail' map of the company like a semi-deserted little branch line on which only a ghost train occasionally ran. So they let the Saint operation run on, underfunded and underplanned, for no realistic planning seemed possible. And, as you already know, that was what I thought too - seven years later in 1986. But fibre optics and satellites were already transforming the telecommunications world; while the Falklands war and developments on Ascension Island had begun to open up unforeseen employment opportunities for young Saints. They would be away from their families and looking for the nearest telephone to call an airport-less island.

On 18th May, 1989, an agreement was signed between the Government of St. Helena and Cable and Wireless for what the company's press release captioned enterprisingly, if less than wholly accurately

DIGITAL FUTURE FOR THE SAINTS

The company was to take over the whole telephone system, internal and international, and spent £1.8 million on a new digital system. There would be world-wide direct dialling through a £1 million satellite link which would provide the island with international facsimile data and automatic telex services from November, 1989.

"Leading Edge Technology" said Tom Chellew for the company, with understandable corporate pride both in the achievement and in the language.

October that year saw the installation at The Briars of the Vista Earth Station ('the dish') which replaced the high frequency and shaky telephone link to Ascension and beyond. In January 1992, seven international channels operated to Ascension; five to the United Kingdom and one to South Africa. A further five channels were to be added in 1992.

A GEC/Plessey digital exchange was installed and cut over on 28th July, 1990 with a capacity of 1,200 lines. The previous PBX had half that. The new exchange was expected to be at full capacity by March, 1992; and a further 900 line expansion was due in service by September, 1992. Underground duct work has replaced overhead cables and provided a web of new telephone links to houses all over St. Helena. The work continues and envisages total capital expenditure of close to £3 million when it is completed.

A new sight for visitors and Saints alike are bright clean phonecard and cash telephone booths scattered at strategic intervals throughout the island: four card and twenty-one coin phone booths are listed in the 1991 directory. Phonecards of £5, £10 and £15 value have attractive scenes of St. Helena chosen by George Stevens. There is no doubt that they will become collectors' items in their own right. Indeed, some say, they already are.

Over all this negotiation and modernisation, George Stevens, a Saint of foresight and determination, has presided with a mixture of pride and perhaps wonder. A dream - his dream - has been realised. For him, St. Helena is no longer at the end of an antiquated line. It already belongs to the telecommunications world of the twenty-first century as part of a fibre optics satellite digital network. And it is far from being a loss leader.

"Look at the traffic figures" said George to me in January, 1992 as he sought to recover from the debilitating flu virus. "Since direct dialling began on 17th January, 1990, international outgoing traffic has grown so fast that we have carried in one month what we used to have in a whole year. No-one - certainly none of us in Cable and Wireless - would have forecast growth remotely to that level. It is truly staggering and it is still growing. We seem to have stumbled on to a moneyspinner."

The new licence to Cable and Wireless for the exclusive operation of St. Helena's national and international services is for twenty-one years. It will thus be due to expire in the year 2010. It would be nice to think that George Stevens and his all-Saint staff will still be around to help negotiate and implement the next one - and, earlier, for the centenary of Cable and Wireless operations on St. Helena in 1999.

I walked one day up to the panoramic heights of High Knoll Fort. Apart from two circling sea birds, I was alone. Or so I thought until I heard the sound of a hammer and faint voices. I went to investigate. Two carpenters were at work. "What is this?" I asked.

"Cable and Wireless transmitter. Air Sea Rescue."

"Ah." I was really none the wiser until I talked again to George Stevens.

"Cable and Wireless has been granted a licence to operate a VHF coast station at High Knoll Fort. The present VHF facilities can only cover the harbour. Fishing boats equipped with VHF facilities, operating at the back of the island, or ships approaching the island from the south, cannot communicate with the coast station. It must be equipped to offer adequate VHF coverage of the whole of St. Helena's coastal waters.

"High Knoll is the best site on which to erect a building for this purpose. Search and Rescue operations which occurred during 1991 - the Saudi Arabian crude oil tanker which exploded and caught fire 470 miles east of St. Helena on 28th May; the *Fairy Tern* which caught fire and sank off the island on 16th August; and the *Oman Sea One* which sank while fishing in our territorial waters on 30th August - were all incidents assisted in by St. Helena's Coast Station at The Briars.

"The new VHF coast station at High Knoll Fort will enable Cable and Wireless to do two things. First, the Search and Rescue authorities ashore, as well as shipping in the immediate vicinity of a ship in distress, will be rapidly alerted so that they can assist in a co-ordinated Search and Rescue operation with the minimum delay. Secondly, the new system will also provide maritime safety information including navigational and meteorological warnings."

There was a Saint on Voyage 6 North who is a self-employed carpenter in Portsmouth. He had been home for the first time in ten years. Except for large tattoo arabesques on both arms, there was less than a remote resemblance to George Stevens.

"Are you a relation of George?" I asked one day as we approached Tenerife.

"No, I'm not. Least not so far I's know." He paused and went on. "You always know you Mummy on St. Helena, but not so sure 'bout you Daddy."

Two buxom Saintly ladies laughed.

"Dat's right," one said. "'Cept you Mummy know. Or t'ink she do."

The 'Digital Future for the Saints' is then not quite so complete. And that is something of a mild relief for those who may still seek to enjoy the freedom of trial and error human experimentation.

Perhaps something of a Collector's Item
(The Ship's maiden voyage began at Cardiff)

CHAPTER 16

Bridge Passage:
Captain Bligh and the Breadfruit

In 1986 I picked up a long slim yellow pamphlet with a black and white sketch of the Castle entrance and an outline map of St. Helena on the front cover. Inside there were maps of upper and lower Jamestown with places of interest to the visitor and an index of their numbers. Another page had a list of 'Significant Dates in the History of St. Helena.' At the bottom of the back page was this:

DRAWN AND COMPILED BY J. DRUMMOND, BRIARS HEIGHTS
Printed at the Government Printing Office, The Castle, St. Helena.
A.A. BIZAARE, Government Printer.

What I found among the 'Significant Dates' may not have been bizarre (or bizaare), but it was certainly unexpected:

1792 Captain Bligh late of *HMS Bounty* visited St. Helena in December. He left five varieties of breadfruit plants, also a quantity of mountain rice seed for cultivation.

At that time, I had not noticed such an entry in other more formidably official lists; nor in other historical summaries. When something like this happens, and you are, by a miracle of good fortune, on St. Helena itself, there is only one place to go: The Castle Archives and the welcoming skills and massive memory of Cecil Maggott.

He is not often non-plussed. This time he was. "No, I didn't know that. So let me see what I can find."

So Cecil Maggott went off into the recesses of his dark and humid storerooms. He re-emerged some minutes later carrying two huge leather-bound volumes. He placed them before me. They occupied nearly all the desk space. I had to stand up to reach the top. When I did so, I found that I had before me in handwritten copperplate the recorded proceedings of the Governing Council of the Honourable East India Company for 1792.

"There" said Cecil Maggott, "you should be able to find confirmation of Captain Bligh's visit to St. Helena."

I am no academic researcher, or practising historian for that matter - as will long since have become apparent to those who have stayed with me so far in this volume. But I was suddenly excited by a discovery, precisely two hundred years after its occurrence. Now you can look at this sort of thing and say disbelievingly to me: how do you know and how do you prove that no-one has discovered much earlier what you say you have yourself first discovered. Answer: I cannot and so I don't intend to try. All I do is to reproduce the 1792 correspondence I found in those volumes; allow it to speak for itself; and share with you the exhilaration I felt at its discovery.

17th December, 1792

At a Consultation held on Monday the 17th day December, 1792 at The Castle -

Present Lieut. Col. Robt. Brooke Governor
Major Francis Robson Lieu' Governor
Willm. Wrangham Esq. of Council

The last Consultation was read, approved, and Signed, dated 10th December, 1792.

This day Arrived his Majesty's Ship PROVIDENCE & Brig AFOISTANT

from the South Seas.

24th December

The Governor addrefsed the Board as follows -
Gentlemen
    Captain Bligh having by his Majesty's goodnefs been directed to touch here with the Breadfruit Tree & has executed his Commifsion to a wish - The Trees he has delivered have been planted under the Directions and advice of Captain Bligh and His Majesty's and the Honble Company's Botanists and in return they have been supplied with all such Plants and Trees from this Island as they wished for - You have seen Gentlemen what order the Garden onboard the Providence was in and the pains taken by Captain Bligh for the Service and I believe you will join with me on thinking we should Publickly acknowledge our feelings upon the occasion.

Signed

R Brooke
Ordered

        Ordered that the following letter be written to Captain Bligh by the Secretary.

    To Capt. Wm. Bligh
        Commanding His Majesty's Ship
          PROVIDENCE
Sir/
I am directed by the Governor and the Council to acknowledge the Receipt of the following Trees and Plants -
    10 Pots and 1 Tub of Bread Fruit Plants very fine
    12 Do sickly -
    2 Pots containing 2 Plants of Avees/Apples

```
1 Do   ------------4 Do     of Rattah/Chesnut
2 Do   -----------3 Do      of Ayyah/Jambo
1 Do   ---------- 1 Do      of Mattee/Trees
1 Do   ---------- 4 Do      of Ettow
2 Do   ----------- 2 Do     of Peeah, besides Roots
                            Timor Plants
1 Pot containing 4 Plants of Nanche/Soursop
1 Do   ------------1 Do     Lemon/China
1 Do   ----------- 2 Jambo mare
1 Do   ----------- 4 Jambo armiriah
1 Do   ------------2 Mango
1 Do   ----------- 2 Penang - /Beetlenut/
1 Do   ----------- 2 - Long Pepper.
1 Do   ----------- 2 ..Black Pepper.
1 Do   ------------1 Buhgnna Banana
```

 The Governor & Council were greatly obliged and highly gratifyed by a view of the Delightful Scene onboard your Ship, which imprefsed their Minds with the warmest and most animated glow of Gratitude towards his Majesty for his Royal Goodnefs, and Benevolent attention shown to the Welfare of his Subjects here and in West India Islands, and it also raised in them an inexprefsible degree of Wonder and Delight to Contemplate a Floating Garden / fraught with what may prove of inestimable value to that part of Mankind who have the Blefsing of residing under his Auspices / transported in luxuriance from one Extremity of the World to the other - at the same time the Board could not help feeling a just sense of Obligation on perceiving how strong an Enthusiast you have been in the Execution of His Majesty's benign Wishes, for it was impofsible not to observe in every part of your Ship the disregard shewn to personal convenience and the Attention and excellent Contrivance displayed in the Accommodation & Preservation of your invaluable Cargo.

 The Board will carefully represent all these Matters home, as also the Attention paid by your Botanists here, and they present you

with their best their best thanks in the name of their Honble
Masters for your kind exertions in every instance to oblige them -

I have the honor to remain
Sir,
Your most Obedient Servant

St. Helena.   *Signed*
24th December 1792   **W.H. Doveton**. *Secry.*

At a Consultation held, on Thursday the 27th Day of December
1792 at The Castle
Present   Lieut. Col. Robt. Brooke Governor
     Major Francis Robson Lieut. Governor
     William Wrangham Esq of Council -
The last Consultation was read, approved and Signed dated the 24th
of December 1792.
  Yesterday Sailed the Genoese Ship Prudent for Ostend. Last
Evening do. His Majesty's Ship Providence & Brig Tender Afoistant
for the West Indies The following Letter was on the 25th instant
Received from Captain Bligh of His Majesty's Ship Providence

To the Honble Governor & Council

St. Helena

 Gentlemen/
 I am now to acknowledge the receipt of your Letter dated
the 24th Instant and to afsure you I am imprefsed with the
Strongest sense of the honorable distinction you have shewn
to me. I shall at every Opportunity in my life be ready to
render service to your Government which our most gracious
King has shewn such a pecular mark of his favor to - May you
live to see a happy result of the labours to serve the Island with
the inestimable Fruits -

I have the honor to be
Gentlemen
Your most Obedient very humble servant

Signed

PROVIDENCE
25 Decembr. 1792   **Wm. Bligh**

And in a report sent to the Company thereafter appeared this:

6 ... Captain Bligh of his Majesty's Ship *Providence* having sent on shore to us a variety of Trees and Plants the Production of the South Seas and Island of Timor We in consequence directed the Secretary to acknowledge their receipt in a Letter entered on Consultation of the 24th inst. to which we beg leave to refer. And also to Captain Bligh's Answer entered upon Consultation of the 27th; Most of these Plants are in high health and we trust will do well - in return we directed Mr. Porteus to furnish His Majesty's Botanists with such Productions of the Island as might be acceptable and gave them every Afsistance and shewed them all the attention in our power..

So there it is. Breadfruit. It was breadfruit for the Caribbean which first took William Bligh and *HMS Bounty* to Tahiti in 1789. This in turn led directly to the infamous mutiny in Tongan internal waters, Bligh's epic open-boat journey to Timor and the founding of the mutineers' settlement on the remote and near-inaccessible island of Pitcairn.

It was breadfruit which took William Bligh back to the South Seas in *HMS Providence*, thence to the South Atlantic East India Company island of St. Helena. And he had called again at Timor, his landfall and point of survival three years before in 1789. That would seem to be a story in itself ...

In Kingstown St. Vincent, there is a notice on an ageing breadfruit tree which commemorates the first such planting there of Tahitian breadfruit by Captain Bligh. Not so on St. Helena. For once St. Helena is silent. There is no public identification of the place where in 1792 that other consignment of breadfruit was planted in its new South Atlantic island home.

BREADFRUIT TREE
(with detail of fruit and foliage)

CHAPTER 17

Past Poetic Licence at Plantation

The Givenchy flooded into the Escort. The car - not the man. For there was no man, yet. Apart from a large one in the front seat. A colonial re-tred: genial, polite and patient. Not without humour and a sense of occasion.

The crown was the magnet. Front and rear of the modest car, parked outside the Consulate Hotel in Jamestown.

"Excuse me."

"Of course."

"You're local, aren' shu? I mean, you live hyah."

The ensemble was impeccable. Perfection at 12° South. And the hair: a conditioned flaky grey. Money oozed from the neckline down. The voice was Cultivated Cultured, the BBC World Service turned up loud. It thrust forward with the scent and was held by it. As was intended.

"Well, yes, I suppose you could say so."

"I mean, I saw the crown. And I thought ..."

"Sometimes things are not what they seem. But can I help you?"

The confidence resurged. High-rise combers but temporarily checked by a swirling undertow.

"Yes. I'd be most grateful. You will know that I came in on the *RMS* with my friend hyah."

"Good morning."

"Good morning."

"Welcome to the island."

"Thank you."

"I hope you enjoy your stay."

"I hope so too. That is what - in a sense - I was speaking about. A moment ago. I was wondering whether you could advise me."

"About what?"

"About, well. About a matter of protocol."

The word gushed forth - PRRROTOCOL.

"It's not my field ... but perhaps my colleague ..."

She ignored him. "I went to Plantation House yesterday."

"Yes." He was resigned now. "The Governor's residence."

"We were anxious to do the right thing, you understand. To ensure that the courtesies were not overlooked. Not to be thought insensitive to the niceties of island decorum. But, well. There was a problem. And that's why we thought, seeing the crown on the car, you wouldn't mind, would you, if we consulted you. Unofficially, that is. You see I know about these things. I was once the Resident in Polynesia. The first. The fact that I was also the only one simply means that the political scene in that vast and complex oceanic world changed so rapidly that we could not fund and set up new posts sufficiently fast to satisfy the nationalistic ambitions of the emerging states of the region. In spite of my advice to the contrary. It is because of my long experience in the South Pacific that, although recently retired, I am now in the South Atlantic seeking to ..."

"Penetrate the mysteries of Plantation House?"

"Yes, exactly. How very perceptive of you. Did you say that you were the ..."

"I didn't. But I happen to be the Colonial Treasurer."

"But I thought ..."

"The crown on the car can be misleading to the visitor when I am driving it." A watery smile. "The shape of things to come perhaps, but not yet."

"Oh splendid. You look to be the type marked out for promotion in the fast stream. I'm a good judge of these things."

"And the problem?"

"Ah, yes. The problem. We went to Plantation House, d'you see, to sign the book in the usual way. But we couldn't find it. And there was no sentry to ask. Very peculiar. There is a book I suppose?"

"Certainly there is. It's in the drawer on the stand inside the shelter opposite the sentry box."

"How very curious. In a drawer. But thank you so much. I knew there must be a book. We shall try again."

And try they did, hiring an open taxi to take them up Ladder Hill, through Half Tree Hollow and past the turn-off for Francis Plain to the entrance to the great and the grand Governor's residence of Plantation House on the island of St. Helena.

Two days later, in Jamestown, they saw the car with the crown again and set off to waylay its driver.

"I think that I ought to tell you so that you may inform His Excellency. If we are to be criticised for lack of courtesy, it will not be **our** fault."

"Oh dear. What went wrong this time?"

"The drawer containing the visitors' book was locked. And though I shook and banged it, I could not get it open. It really was aggravating, after all the trouble we had taken. And we now have so little time left - before the ship sails. Do you think it at all possible for you to mention to His Excellency that we did try to do the correct thing but for reasons beyond our control ..."

"Certainly, I will. I am sure that the Governor will be most concerned, particularly since he has such a busy schedule of engagements at this time of year."

The Colonial Treasurer turned away, started the sluggish engine of the diesel Escort and moved off. It wasn't for him to tell them that the Governor's standing orders were that the visitors' book at the gates of Plantation House was always to be locked in the drawer when the monthly Royal Mail Ship was in James Bay. It was the only way he could be protected from the social climbers, the inquisitive and the free drink seekers who trekked up from the town hoping to get inside the old East India Company's pride and joy, to find Jonathan the aged tortoise or perhaps, just perhaps, to be asked to tennis and cocktails.

Then, as the departing three blasts from the siren of the old *RMS St. Helena* rolled around the steep and stark hillsides above Jamestown, the Governor would take the key from his pocket and hand it to the butler.

"The drawer can be opened again now, George.   For another month." And George would think 'His Ex. sure know a t'ing or two' and would dutifully do as he was bidden.

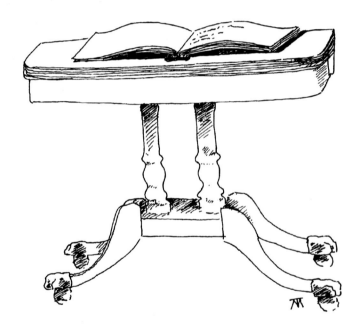

CHAPTER 18

Island of Exile

The Zulus

Napoleon Bonaparte was not the only prisoner of war - or something akin to it - to be exiled to St. Helena. There were others who were despatched to detention in the Citadel of the South Atlantic. In 1889, Prince Dinuzulu and his two uncles, Ndabuko and Shingana, were convicted in Zululand of taking part in a rebellion against Queen Victoria. They were shipped to St. Helena and arrived at the island on 25th February, 1890, accompanied by four women, two of whom were single friends of Dinuzulu and the others a wife of each of the chiefly uncles. There were four male attendants, one being a native doctor.

'Dinuzulu,' said the weekly *St. Helena Guardian*, 'is a sweet looking young fellow ... and came on shore wearing gaiters and carried in his hand a riding whip. Although an exile, he still maintains his dignity and messes by himself, his two uncles having their meals at a different table. The women almost crawled out of the boat upon landing ... The two unmarried ladies have accepted the protection of His Zulu Highness during his sojourn on the island ...'

Unsurprisingly, it was not very long before 'protection' turned out to be something rather different. In hand-written despatches to the Right Honourable Lord Knutsford of 10th and 17th September, 1890, Governor W. Grey Wilson had

'the honour to transmit copies of letters with reference to two of the women of the Zulu establishment being *enceinte*. It will be seen that I have discouraged any hope that the request preferred for the return of the women to Zululand will be entertained; but I have consented upon the solicitation of the Guardian to submit the matter for your Lordship's consideration ... I reproached the Prisoners with not having revealed the

state of these two women while Mr. Saunders (the white Guardian) was
here, and they replied that it was not possible as no Zulu woman dare
disclose her condition to her husband and they had only just found it out
when they told me.

I am sending Sir Charles Mitchell (Governor of Zululand) a copy of the
enclosures hereto and I shall suggest for his consideration the propriety
of sending to St. Helena a Zulu midwife for the present and future need.
Upon the question of the sufficiency of the food supply, I sometime ago
asked Sir Charles Mitchell's opinion, my own being that the enormous
consumption of castor oil and other purgatives (by the Zulu prisoners)
seems rather to indicate a too generous diet coupled with extreme
slothfulness.'

In the event and upon the urgings of the Guardian and the Lord
Bishop, the Governor consented 'to send home Itlazile and an
attendant at government expense with the two women *enceinte*
provided the chiefs themselves paid the passages of the two latter ...
on the ground of it being a Zulu religious rite ... without waiting for
Sir Charles Mitchell's opinion.'

For the next four years, the Governor's despatches contain regular
quarterly and health reports on the Zulus. Then, on 7th July 1893 and
12th February and 8th March, 1895, the despatch subject is

Zulu Chiefs ask to see Queen

Grey Wilson sent forward the Zulu petition but made no recom-
mendation in respect of it; and nothing came of it. Indeed, it was not
until mid-1897 that the Governor received instructions that the Zulu
chiefs and their by now enlarged entourage were to be repatriated.
They duly embarked for Natal on the *S.S. Umbilo*, 1,232 tons, on
24th December, 1897, seven years and ten months after their arrival.

Governor R.A. Sterndale reported the departure of 'Dinuzulu,
Ndabuko and Shingana with their wives, children and attendants in
all 25 souls. With them went Mr. Madden the Guardian and Daniel
the interpreter ...' In that despatch of 1st February, 1898, Sterndale

made no observations about the circumstances of repatriation or the condition or reactions of the Zulus. His concern appeared to be solely that 'their departure is a loss financially to the island as over £1,500 a year was spent on rations and clothing, and several of the island officials' (including himself) 'got a slight increase to their small salaries on account of duties performed which of course have now ceased ...'

THE BOERS

The consequences of past wars in far off lands for the island and people of St. Helena are not confined to the Napoleonic wars in Europe and the exile of the former French Emperor. The 1899-1902 Boer War in South Africa led to the despatch to St. Helena of about 6,000 Boer prisoners. The first detachment of 514 arrived in the *Milwaukee* on 14th April, 1900. It included the defeated Boer General Cronje whom *Punch* depicted saluting the ghost of Napoleon and saying 'Same enemy, sire. Same result.' The rest came in twelve different ships between then and February, 1902; and were held in two camps - Deadwood Plain in the eastern part of the island and Broad Bottom in the west. A third camp contained prisoners who wanted to become British. These men called themselves 'Loyalists' and were held in the so-called Peace Camp. The other prisoners dubbed them 'Traitors.'

Repatriation to South Africa took place between June and October, 1902. Some of the prisoners failed to return home. The Knollcombes Boer cemetery on St. Helena has 156 numbered graves set in regimented rows. They have been visited, tended and honoured by naval and other detachments from South Africa; and remain a source of nostalgic interest to present-day visitors from the Republic. The Government of St. Helena's Custodian of Records says in a note dated 28th April, 1987:

THE BOER CEMETERY at KNOLLCOMBES
The two Memorials are engraved with the names of 180 Boers
said to range in age from 16 to 74

ABOVE THE CEMETERY TO THE RIGHT IS THE
BAPTIST CHURCH
with burial ground and Memorial to Hudson Ralph Janisch - Governor 1873

'Amongst the prisoners were musicians, teachers, architects, carpenters etc., and many of these obtained employment with farmers and merchants, who were responsible for them in working hours.'

The Custodian of Records at the Archives of the Government of St. Helena is Cecil Maggott. It is a pity that his name is thus so joke-prone because his spectacular memory and painstaking help and courtesy to scholars, researchers and casual visitors is dedicated and perhaps unique. At 57, he has been twenty five years in the post. His sole formal preparation for it was a visit in 1965 to the Public Records Office in London.

"Our archives go back to 1680," he says. "We have intact all the records of the East India Company until 1910; but we have no military records and most of the civil ones from 1900-1965 have apparently been lost ... I sometimes wonder about the succession here. I have had five different assistants since 1978. They last a couple of years and then move on. Can't blame them I suppose ..." A tale of lamentation that, sadly, one hears from so many communities as we near the end of the century...

It was not quite the end of St. Helena as an island of exile. In 1957 three Bahraini subjects were brought for detention. They had been prominent members of a so-called committee of nationalists in Bahrain. They had been convicted before the court of the Ruler of Bahrain for offences against the state and sentenced to four years imprisonment. The Ruler had asked for their removal to a British territory - a nice example of passing the buck; and the decision to send them to the unprotesting Saints was effected by the device of applying the Colonial Prisoners Removal Act of 1869 to Bahrain by Order of Her Majesty in Council.

A similar recourse in the case of Archbishop Makarios of Cyprus at about the same time was considered and dropped. The Seychelles received him instead, at the height of EOKA terrorism in Cyprus.

CHAPTER 19

Father Christmas

At the end of January 1992, the *RMS* set off on the shuttle to Ascension. Again I stayed on St. Helena, this time at Cleughs Plain.

"Where?" they asked.

"Cleughs Plain."

"Cleughs Plain?"

"Yes."

"But no one lives on Cleughs Plain. Well, almost no one. Who with?"

"With Julie and Malvin Lawrence."

"They don' have space."

"Well they made it. Their seven year old son Ricky moved out of his bedroom and I moved in - among the shoes and the clothes and the toys and the games and the wall decorations. It was a bit of a squeeze, if you add in the dog and the cat and the pig and the queue for the bathroom; but it was fine. And I tell you, when at the end of the day she has stopped being Registrar of the Supreme Court, all bewigged and black-gowned, Julie is no mean cook. Even without her temperamental microwave. And Malvin is developing a fine vegetable garden in between building houses."

"Oh. So it was all right then?"

"Yes. It was."

"You survived?"

"Yes."

"Oh."

I hired a car from Belfred McDaniel who has a body shop of the vehicular kind tucked away among the old fortifications of Ladder Hill. It was a reconstituted - recycled perhaps - Ford Escort of indeterminate vintage.

"I bought it as a wreck," he said "and put it all together again. It goes fine. You won't have any trouble."

"Can I take it down Sandy Bay hill do you think?"

"Sure. No problem."

Little did I know. I signed a piece of paper which required me to check the oil and the water and tyres and the battery daily. Now that seemed odd, but my education into St. Helena car number 240 was just beginning.

There was a towel spread from side to side above the dashboard.

"What's that for?" I asked.

"The rain. Comes through the windscreen. Pull the mats back on the floorboards and you'll see I've drilled a hole through the metal so that water can escape. The left hand door doesn't shut too well. You need to give it a good push from the outside. But don't worry. The brakes are OK. And get some petrol straight away. You pay for that."

I looked again at the typed paper. It said something obscure about insurance.

"Who pays for that?"

"Oh. No charge. Just £8 a day for the car. That's a good deal." So David Clarke had said too when he found the car for me.

It was painted in garish red and white. I promptly christened it Father Christmas. I might well need to call on the reindeer. In seven days Father Christmas conveyed me over 141 miles of the daunting roads of St. Helena. No big deal: except that on only two occasions did I consider it practicable and sensible to flirt briefly with the heady excitements of top gear.

* * *

Stedson Stroud and Vilma Henry are a couple whose deeds reflect their words. He is 42, she 35; and both are non-meat eaters. They live at Cedar Vale on Thompson's Hill, about ten miles from Jamestown.

It is another world. For me, it was the end of the line across the mountain ridges from Cleughs Plain to Rosemary Plain; then the jagged bends to High Point, deep falls on both sides; along the contour line to Thompson's Hill where, silent and enveloped in rich tropical vegetation, the road gave up. Up to the left was a steep entrance to a half-hidden solitary house. In a garage a huge old Landrover - and a smiling Stedson, in jeans, work shirt and knee boots on the roadside.

"So you found us all right?"

"Yes, thank God. Quite a journey."

A man of property and of the land grasped my hand. And then, like Alice, I stepped through the looking glass and into a St. Helenian wonderland. Inside, an elegant Vilma, black eyes and hair aglow, was surrounded by a galaxy of interior greenery and pot plants, floor to ceiling. In house, garden and sheds, there were more than two hundred varieties of St. Helena flora in seed, pots and plants - radiant bougainvillaea, cactus, ferns, fuschias, coleus, begonias, peach, granadillas, passion fruit, pawpaw, bananas, nectarines, oranges, figs and more.

All this is Vilma's domain and responsibility. The rest is Stedson's. His principal interest is honey. His production is about 1,000 lbs. in a summer season of three months. Extraction is by what he calls 'the old method.' The combs are crushed with a large wooden spoon in a bucket, then filtered through gauze to produce liquid and comb honey from the wild flowers of St. Helena. It is, he says, very smooth, light in colour and does not go hard. It crystallizes into its creamy texture and is neither sweet nor sharp. Indeed its unusual taste is its particular quality. Stedson Stroud packs his honey for Britain and Ascension Island, for the stores of Jamestown and the countryside and for the ship's shop on the *RMS*. There you can buy it with its colourful label.

Also at Cedar Vale you will find six cows for breeding beef, six goats and fifteen sheep, also for breeding. Activity is everywhere in this rustic retreat. What came before is equally enterprising.

For six year, from 1970 to 1976, Stedson lived in England. He was assistant butler and then butler at Weston Park, the stately home of the Earl and Countess of Bradford, near Wolverhampton. Then he went to France, the village of Dreux in Normandy. There at the Chateau St. George he filled a similar rôle for the Comtesse de la Veldene from 1976 to 1981. She was, he says, a cousin of Winston Churchill who married a French count.

During both these periods, Stedson had opportunities for travel, both with his respective employers and on his own. He took every one. The cosseted comfort of high life limousines and jacuzzis in New York and Palm Beach was matched by 'backpacking' all over the Middle East, north and south in Europe, South Africa, Mauritius, Hong Kong, Australia and North Africa.

"For fourteen years from 1967 to 1981," says Stedson, "I would just put some money in my pocket, a pack on my back, buy a ticket and set off to the first destination. Thereafter I went wherever chance took me."

Chance took a hand again when he heard in 1981 that the old *RMS St. Helena* was about to go off on duty as a naval support ship in the Falklands war and was wanting additional St. Helenian crew. He signed on and has been with Curnow Shipping and the *RMS* - old and new - ever since. When they are not off duty at Cedar Vale, Stedson is a dining saloon steward and Vilma a cabin stewardess. No passenger could begin to guess the nature of their 'other life'; or that, without question, Stedson Stroud is the World's Most Travelled Saint. And thankfully one of the most modest.

"So what, on the *RMS*," I asked, "do you like least?"

"Passengers who look through you rather than at you."

Again, he had replied without hesitation. Again, because it was Stedson Stroud who, in the dining saloon of the *RMS* on Voyage 6 South, had described St. Helena, for him, as 'paradise.' I could now see why. He and Vilma had created it by their own efforts.

For me it was different as I set off mid-afternoon in the seat-beltless 240 on what was said to be a fifteen to twenty minute journey.

My destination was Blue Hill and the residence of Ruth and Gordon Pridham. Ruth is a qualified and experienced teacher who worked in Britain for many years before heading home with her husband. She was until 1993 a member of the Territory's Executive Council, the Chairman of the Education Committee and a long-standing elected member of the Legislative Council.

"Just follow the signs," they said as I set off. "It's easy."

Well, I suppose it might have been if the weather had not taken a nose dive into swirling mists and ghastly gloom and if Father Christmas had not decided to be bloody-minded.

I got to Rosemary Plain and White Gate all right and was setting off to the high junction for Sandy Bay when the radiator started to fizzle and spurt. Then the windscreen wipers gave up; the horn abandoned tootability at hairpin bends; the fuel and temperature gauges got jammed, immobile, at zero; and then the rains came. I got out of the car and promptly slipped on the mud at the edge of the cliff. I sat down abruptly and dropped my cabin door key into the swirling cascade as I reached for a damp handkerchief. It had become suddenly dark. I turned the switch on the lights so that I could find the key. They didn't work either. "It's all very well for you," I said to the absent Stedson, "in your blasted paradise and great Landrover!"

It took me fifty-five minutes to get to Blue Hill after I had found a sawmill, put some water in the radiator and, with help, got the wipers wiping. For sixty seconds. Then they expired again. My head out of the window, muddied shoes slipping off and on clutch, break and accelerator at the wrong moment, Father Christmas and I made walking pace progress, not a reindeer in sight.

"You all right?" asked Ruth. The second time I had heard it that day.

"Yes," I said, shaking, as I told them half the story. "Piece of cake, really."

"Well that's what I've made for you. Have some tea and relax."

By five o'clock it was becoming more gloomy still. The mists were thickening. But the engine started. That was something. I set off again and found the comforting red tail lights of a PWD truck heading for Jamestown. Hooter blaring, light flashing, it got me through the worst. Now I know what it's like as a sucker fish to hitch a ride on a large shark.

By the time I reached the top of Half Tree Hollow the weather was behind me, the Atlantic Ocean stretched away below in infinite splendour and I was in the golden rays of a setting sun. It was, as they say, another South Atlantic world; and the release into light of the prisoners in Beethoven's *Fidelio*. I drove into the dusty recesses of the body shop at Ladder Hill, turned off the engine, breathed again, and got out. Father Christmas looked the worse for wear. So did I.

Belfred McDaniel came out, wiping his hands.

"You're back then. Everything OK?"

"No. I'm afraid it wasn't and I'm not ..." Then I began to shake with relieved and relaxed laughter. A reconstructed wreck. Sure was; but what the hell. So was I; and I was in one piece. So I told the story. Briefly.

"Oh. Fuse gone, I suppose. Let's look. Yeah. This one's a bit loose. There you are."

In thirty seconds, the windscreen wipers worked again. The gauges moved to their right places. The horn rang out loud and clear. The lights came on and off ... And water?

"Yeah. Think I'll have to replace that radiator. Gotta leak, this one. So down to the landing and the *RMS* now I suppose?"

My packed suitcases were in the boot. They were miraculously intact and dry.

"Yes, please."

"You drive?"

"No. I'll leave Father Christmas to you now and be happy to go down Ladder Hill Road as his passenger on our last journey together."

The reconstituted Ford Escort conveyed me safely down through the walled intricacies and hazards of Ladder Hill Road. For no apparent reason, I suddenly remembered an advertisement I saw years ago in the Do-It-Yourself advertising section of a New Zealand newspaper:

MAKE YOUR OWN GENUINE ANTIQUE FURNITURE

Maybe that singular concept had caught on in St. Helena. For motor cars.

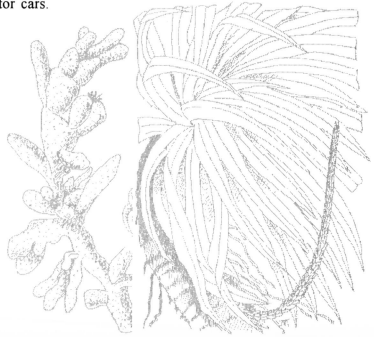

CHAPTER 20

The Has and the Has Nots

I sat on the sun deck of the *RMS* one day en route to Tristan and played a little game. I put down all the 'has nots' I could think of in respect of St. Helena - all those things that the island does not enjoy or suffer. Then I listed what the island does have, good or not so good.

Here are the lists in no particular or logical sequence.

THE HAS NOTS OF ST. HELENA

No pollution
No organised crime
No cases of robbery with violence
No stabbings or shootings or muggings
No airport
No mass tourism
No two, three, four or five star hotels
No commercialisation of Longwood or The Briars
No public transport system
No racial or religious hatred or aggression
No riots or arson
No manifest corruption on the part either of politicians or
    public servants
No true poverty
No slums
No beggars or touts
No known prostitution
No case of AIDS - yet
No television
No absence of adequate care for the aged, the disturbed and
    children from broken homes

No racial or social prejudices

No Chinese takeaway

No McDonald's or Kentucky Fried Chicken

No Asian restaurant

No indigenous cultural inheritance in song, dance, art or
national dress

No sustained high humidity and thus no serious corrosion or
rusting of motor vehicles and machinery

No malaria or other insect borne diseases

No wild animals

No poisonous insects or other creatures

No cocaine, hashish, opium or crack

No language other than (sort of) English

No full British passport, thus ...

No automatic right of entry to Britain

No commercial bank and thus ...

No overdrafts, cheque books or credit cards

No exchange controls

No traffic lights, parking meters, traffic wardens or wheel clamping

No motorways or motor racing circuits

No capital gains tax

No succession or inheritance tax, in practice, for almost everyone

No postal delivery service

No lawyers, architects or accountants in private practice

No ice or snow

No neon signs or billboards

No vandalism

No graffiti

No earthquakes (since 1817), hurricanes or (virtually) thunderstorms

No horse racing and no horses

No Mormons

No optician

No orthopaedic surgeon

No mineral resources

No sex shops

No proper port or harbour facilities

THE HAS OF ST. HELENA

A kind, gentle, courteous and hospitable people
A great community spirit, the epitome of domestic cleanliness
    and concern for the appearance of streets and houses
The *RMS St. Helena*
A variety of religious persuasions - Anglican, Roman Catholic,
    Baptist, Salvation Army, Seventh Day Adventist,
    Bahai, Jehovah's Witnesses
Freedom of speech and religious worship
An open sense of humour and fun
An historically fascinating racial inheritance
A restiveness among the young that seems to be no more and
    no less than that of other societies
A good medical and public health service, but ...
A revitalised three tier education structure and schools;
    resourcefulness in isolation in spite of the Education
    Department address being 'The Canister'
A reliable, if expensive, electricity supply
A splendid piped water supply and reservoirs
A bulk fuel storage farm
A fisheries enterprise and fresh tuna canning factory
A benign climate with no extremes
A world-wide instant direct dial satellite telephone system and
    the FAX
Radio St. Helena, a community radio station of the best kind
    which relays the BBC World Service by day Monday
    to Friday with local programmes at night and does all
    this in swirling mists most days
A responsive and dedicated social services network
Independence of the judiciary and the courts
A system of lay advocates to assist the accused in charges
    before the courts and lay magistrates in the lower courts

A bevy of bright-eyed attractive women customs and police officers
The wirebird
Historical and architectural riches
Open archives
Philatelic integrity
'Calling of the Mail'
A golf course
Computers
Videomania
Low income tax
Decaying fortresses and fortifications
The Ladder
Loyalty to the British Royal Family, with photographs in
    most homes
Annual budgetary aid and shipping subsidy from London
A tradition of fine quality stonemasonry
The oceanic isolation to enable St. Helena so far to protect its
    precious assets
The last years of Napoleon Bonaparte 1815-1821
Too many smokers
An apparently unlimited supply of Castle lager from South Africa

I came to an exhausted pause at this point and showed the lists to
Alan and Delia Hoole. They added:

Unique flora and fauna
Sports - skittles (No. 1), cricket, soccer, shooting, tennis,
    squash, fishing
Fascinating geology
Excellent walks
Self sufficiency in timber
Boer and Zulu prisoners (in the past)
Stable currency - the pound sterling
Stability under the British flag

And, I thought, above all a justified pride in being a Saint.

So those are the two lists, put together as a sort of parlour - or in this case, shipboard - game. But a serious attempt, nonetheless, at summarised accuracy. See whether you can add to them. I can think of one or two more already.

* * *

CABLE & WIRELESS

ST HELENA

FACSIMILE

Cable and Wireless plc
PO Box 2
The Briars
St. Helena Island
South Atlantic Ocean

Int. Tel: +290 2211
Nat. Tel: 2211
Fax: 2213

Cable and wireless plc
ST. HELENA

TELEPHONE
DIRECTORY

March 1992
Third Edition

CHAPTER 21

Oman Sea One

Have you ever stared death in the face? It is, say those who have, a more than sobering experience. This is a story of one man who did; and of others, from the *RMS St. Helena* and from the island itself who came almost as close. It is not least a story of men who lived when others died; and whose survival came about in yet another strange tale of the raging sea. It is a story that stays on in the minds and hearts of the officers and crew of the *RMS*; for the nobility of rescue from terminal danger forges an enduring bond between rescuer and rescued ...

On the afternoon of Friday, 3rd August, 1991, the *RMS* anchored off Jamestown on Voyage 4 South. She was six hours behind schedule having encountered severe weather from ahead for almost the whole of the two day journey from Ascension Island. Caught in the same conditions was another vessel, a tiny factory trawler of only 290 GRT which had recently started crab fishing around Ascension, St. Helena and the surrounding sea mounts. About four years old, she was owned by an Anglo-Omani consortium and was in fine condition after an extensive refit. She was air-conditioned with an array of the most modern of navigational and technological aids. Her name: *Oman Sea One*.

Twenty four hours after her arrival at St. Helena, the *RMS* had discharged the last of her southbound cargo and was about to load for Cape Town before sailing south that night. Then it was that Radio Officer Bob Wilson, monitoring St. Helena Radio ZHH, picked up the news that a Panamanian-registered tanker *Ruth M*, en route from Chile to Angola, had come upon two liferafts some ninety nautical miles north-west of St. Helena in the vast expanses of the South Atlantic Ocean. In one liferaft were nine men. In the second there were three. All twelve were survivors from the *Oman Sea One* which had foundered in the storm at about dawn the previous day. Those rescued included all the Saints among the crew of seventeen and the British Chief Officer Cyril 'Spud' Cudd from Salcombe in Devon. Five others were missing. They included the Master.

"It all happened so fast. At 6 a.m. I was in my bunk," says Spud. "The Captain was on watch. If it had been slow, he would have called me. One minute I was in bed. Thirty seconds later, we were fighting for our lives. The ship just turned over. The Captain opened the accommodation door and green water poured in. He was sucked out as air and water fought. I never saw him again ... He was a pal of mine ... We don't really know what happened ... Maybe a seacock blew ... The strange thing is that the tanker which picked us up had just changed course to avoid a bit of bad weather. Otherwise they would have missed us and I wouldn't be here now."

That Saturday afternoon on the last day of August, 1991, the reality of his constitutional responsibilities for shipping was borne in on Governor Alan Hoole. From The Castle in Jamestown he took charge of and co-ordinated an air-sea rescue operation remote from the main shipping and air lanes of the world. At four o'clock, with some passengers on board and some not, the *RMS* weighed anchor and set off for the disaster area at maximum speed with 100% engine power. Two hours out, she passed the *Ruth M* inward bound for St. Helena with the survivors. Then, at 1820, a United States Air Force P3 Orion, responding to the call for aerial search assistance, reported sighting the bow of the *Oman Sea One* and a solitary liferaft thirteen miles north-west of the wreck.

Working up to eighteen knots and guided by flares dropped by the Orion, the *RMS* reached the scene at 2230. The little fishing vessel was largely submerged but still afloat. Some twenty five feet of the bow pointed vertically up from the water. "It looked just like a shark's tooth" says Chief Officer Bob Hone.

'Weather conditions were very poor' wrote Captain Bob Wyatt in his report. 'The wind was south-easterly force 8 with rain showers. We were pitching heavily. Spray and water were breaking over the wreck. There was no visible sign of life.'

With search lights ablaze, the *RMS* began a series of passes and sweeps which were to go on throughout the stormy night. The Orion set off for Ascension when its fuel began to run low. A Cyprus-registered freighter *Padrone* joined the search. Normal watches and sleep were abandoned. The bridge of the *RMS* was tense and grim. Bob Wyatt dossed down there for an hour or two. His report takes up the story again, early Sunday morning:

> 0400 We thought the bow section of the *Oman Sea One* was lower in the water. Still vertical, but only 15 to 20 feet visible. The weather was showing signs of moderating. I estimated the wind at south-easterly force 5/4; but still with a nasty sea and swell running.
>
> 0545 It was now noticeable that the bow was slowly settling.
>
> 0558 Lost radar contact, but still had visual contact if one knew where to look and kept to the edge of the searchlight beam. Otherwise the reflection of the spray and rain obscured vision. We were making about 0.2 knot against the weather, two to three hundred feet off the hulk.
>
> 0602 Bow one foot clear of the surface.

Fate or luck then took a hand. "For some reason" says Bob Wilson, "I was looking in the wrong direction - that is astern of the ship - when I saw something glinting in the water. It looked like an old paint tin perhaps and certainly not like a lifejacket at that stage. I alerted the Captain who decided to bring the ship round in a great arc while I tried to keep my eye on the object as best I could in the rise and fall of the ship. It seemed an age before we got back close enough to see that it was indeed a lifejacket."

"It was all in the grey semi-light before sunrise," recalls the officers' cabin steward Michael Francis. "The searchlights picked up flashes from the reflectors of a lifejacket amid all the debris and oil on the surface of the sea. At that stage it was impossible to tell whether there was anyone in it, let alone whether he was alive or dead if there was."

"Then suddenly," says Bob Wilson, "a figure sprang into life and began to wave like crazy."

"The atmosphere on the crowded bridge was now one of deadly seriousness," recalls Bob Hone. "There was none of our occasional banter. We were tense and silent, and kept going on continuous cups of coffee. Now we were facing the prospect of life or death for one survivor. What happened to him was in our hands."

Wyatt began to manoeuvre the ship to create a lee for the launch of the rescue boat. In it were Chief Officer Bob Hone with Second Mate Rodney Young, Third Engineer David Yon and Bosun Pat Williams of St. Helena with sailor Julian Swain of Tristan da Cunha. All were in survival suits.

"I can remember that horrible period," Bob Hone grimly reflects "of sitting in the driver's seat of No. 2 boat ready and waiting for the order to go. It seemed like an hour but I suppose it was only twenty minutes or so. Anyhow at last the Captain said 'Down you go.' So we lowered the boat, pulled the lever, started the engine and put her into gear. Leaving the ship was not difficult; but the next minute we were out in the middle of the ocean pitching up and down a good eighteen feet I guess. We went up and up and up. Looking ahead, we could see nothing but the top of the wave. Then down and down; and from the trough we could only just see the top of the funnel of the *RMS*. There was a stream of instructions from the bridge directing us to the survivor. At first, we couldn't see him either, of course.

"Then after about ten minutes we spotted him from the crest of the swell looking very bedraggled. Rodney Young grabbed the megaphone and gave the classic order: 'Don't move. Stay where you are!'... As if the guy was going to jump out of his life jacket at that stage ... But it relieved the tension a bit.

"The first time past we managed to gaff him with a boathook; and with one great heave we got him on board-like a big fish. He lay there head down over the gunwale, water cascading off him. He was covered in a film of diesel oil, his eyes completely glazed, petrified in shock ..."

"And sheer exhaustion, I suppose?"

"No, no ... It was much more than that." Bob Hone looks

reflective. "They talk about being face to face with God. It was something like that. Imagine: in those conditions he had spent forty-eight hours alone in an air lock in the fo'c'sle head of a small ship which was sinking. He had no idea what was going on. He was the cook - his first ever time at sea. It was his ignorance that kept him where he was. He had been totally petrified - and who wouldn't be? He saw our searchlights, opened a hatch and jumped into the sea. How he managed to do it, I don't know. The will to live ...?"

With the air released and its last remaining buoyancy gone, the end was close. Minutes later, at 0606, the *Oman Sea One* finally expired. The bow section disappeared and the little crab fishing vessel sank into the embrace of the South Atlantic Ocean.

Raphael Dalmeida from India was plucked into the lifeboat of the *RMS St. Helena* at 0700 on Sunday, 1st September, 1991; but the boat had yet to be recovered by the ship. To do so took forty minutes and three attempts. All were hazardous in the conditions and demanded seamanship of a high order on ship and boat. For Bob Hone and his rescue crew it was the toughest and most gruelling task of all.

"First of all, I had to turn round. It was not easy in that swell. We would go up, see the ship; go down again, not see the ship. We got round the stern as the captain made a lee by staying beam on to the swell. The ship was rolling about 20° and here we were with a new ship and a new lifeboat - new to us I mean - coming in under the davits. They were swinging out about twenty feet or so away from the ship's side. Then, as the ship rolled back down the swell, they would smash against the steelwork, making a hell of a noise. As the generators were going, the ship was pushing out about a ton or so of water every five minutes and we had to contend with that too.

"On the first run we didn't quite get the hooks in properly. So I backed off. We had only about thirty seconds to get it right or we would batter the lifeboat and ourselves to pieces against the ship's side as she rolled away. The second run had to be aborted too. I called the captain on the VHF and said: 'I don't think we can make it with the ship lying beam to the swell. We are going to have to head into the wind and try to come in when the ship is pitching.'

"So it was agreed, but this was far from easy too. The boat was pitching like crazy. We made it on our third approach when the captain had turned the ship half into the swell to give us some protection. All the time I had to steer with my head out of the cowling window and the fall blocks shooting past my head. They are about twelve inches square and weigh a fair old whack. A clout from one of them and you would know all about it ...

"We finally got things tied and I shouted 'heave away.' Bang, bang and we were up to the embarkation deck. I could only think: we've arrived, we've done it, all I want is a cigarette ... By this time, the survivor was looking round and trying to smile as he realised where he was. The doctor took him over. I slumped against a canopy. Suddenly I went limp and started to shake. I was like a piece of jelly. It must have been because the job was done, the men were safe and the responsibility was no longer mine. So the tension was released.

"I took the two lifejackets from the *Oman Sea One* up to the bridge and then went down to my cabin. There I found my wife asleep. I said I'm sorry but I think I have besmirched me breeches dear ..."

Bob Hone and I laughed.

"But it was good to have saved a life. That guy would have died. Yet I was really tested. The conditions were awesome. I had never before taken a lifeboat away in deep sea. It seemed a hell of a huge ocean to get lost in ..."

I turned again to Captain Bob Wyatt's report for Sunday, 1st September, 1991:

0740 Lifeboat recovered after three attempts to get alongside the ship. The vessel was then manoeuvred slowly away from the wreckage and once clear of the flotsam speed increased to nine knots. Reported from the survivor that there was no one else alive on the wreck.

A second American search aircraft arrived on the scene during the rescue and continued to circle the ship, while the rescue was in progress. For the aircraft we estimated the surface drift at two knots. Full reports being given to the aircraft as obtained from the survivor. The aircraft then used a base vector of 300° true, for a distance from the wreck of 43 nautical miles, twenty-five miles either side of the vector course in flight paths two miles apart at a height of 500 feet to resume the search. Reports were also given to St. Helena radio and also received from St. Helena from the other survivors who had already been landed at St. Helena.

The *M.V. Padrone* was at that time steaming towards us. I asked her master to take station one mile to the north of us on our starboard side. On a course of 300° true, speed nine knots, this he did.

0920 Liferaft sighted ahead and between both vessels. *Padrone* to close, investigate and retrieve if possible. Master agreed. We then moved further north to search for a lifebuoy sighted by the search aircraft.

1135 *Padrone* reports that she had recovered an unused twenty-five man liferaft. The recovery of this liferaft accounts for the three liferafts carried by the *Oman Sea One*.

1140 Sent a message to *Padrone* releasing her from the search, in view of her shortage of bunkers, to continue her passage to New York. As we steamed back towards our datum point, the sinking position of the *Oman Sea One*, we sighted lifejackets, lifebuoy, several fishing floats and other flotsam, no survivors.

1315 American search aircraft closed the vessel and informed us that they were at the end of their endurance range. They gave us their search area report and departed for base.

1700 Spoke to Governor Hoole to update him and to tell him all that we had gleaned from the survivor. Governor Hoole had medical advice that survivors in the sea in the prevailing conditions and a sea temperature of 20.5°C might still be alive. The search was to continue for a further twenty-four hours until sunset Monday, 2nd September. Using the oil slick from the *Oman Sea One* as our datum point, we carried out an expanding squared search of the area. Throughout the whole of the search period there were never less than five lookouts on duty and for most of the time considerably more, as off duty officers and crew members from all departments, most passengers and all officers' wives acted as extra lookouts...

At 1800 on Monday, 2nd September, exactly twenty four hours later, the *RMS* passed through the oil slick for the last time. Apart from a little floating debris, nothing further was sighted. At 1839 the search was abandoned. The ship arrived back at St. Helena at 0100 on Tuesday, 3rd September. The new *RMS*, her officers and crew had come of age. But they had not been alone.

"The American aircraft crews deserve the highest praise for their efficiency in directing us" says Radio Officer Bob Wilson.

"The one thing that amazed me" Chief Purser Colin Dellar recalls "was the response of the American air and sea rescue from West Africa. Relays of Orion aircraft flew to Ascension refuelled and swept the area of the disaster countless times before the search was finally abandoned. And it was all done with such calm efficiency. Without that, we might never have located the sinking vessel."

The *RMS* sailed for Cape Town on 3rd September with seven of the survivors on board. Of the total complement of seventeen on board the *Oman Sea One*, thirteen survived and four were lost: the British Master, two engineers and deckhand.

On 6th September, 1991, the Governor of St. Helena sent this fax to the Managing Director of Curnow Shipping in Porthleven, Cornwall.

♔

PLANTATION HOUSE,
ISLAND OF ST. HELENA,
SOUTH ATLANTIC OCEAN.

Mr A Bell   Ref CO 150/15
The Shipyard
Porthleven   6 September 1991
Helston
Cornwall
TR13 9JA
United Kingdom

Dear Mr Bell

SEARCH FOR SURVIVORS FROM VESSEL OMAN SEA ONE

1. I write formally to thank Curnow Shipping Ltd, and in particular Captain Bob Wyatt, for the invaluable assistance rendered to the St Helena Government in the search for survivors of the crab fishing vessel Oman Sea One from 31 August until 2 September.

2. As a result of their efforts one life has been saved and we have been able to gather together a considerable amount of additional information on the tragedy.

3. Captain Wyatt reported his actions to Executive Council on Tuesday and gave a radio interview which was broadcast on Wednesday. His description of the rescue operation was clear, concise and moving. It served to remind us all of the perils of the sea.

4. Will you please convey my personal thanks to Captain Wyatt and all the officers and crew of the RMS St Helena who were involved in the operation.

Yours sincerely

A N Hoole
Governor

CHAPTER 22

A Swain of Tristan

I first saw him on the foredeck of the *RMS* in Cardiff. A biting
wind had rattled and shaken the Severn Bridge as we drove over it.
Now the rain swirled round the swimming pool and the sun deck.
Andrew Bell pointed him out to me. He was working in the open. He
didn't seem to notice the wind and rain - or the unfriendly temperature.

"He is our one Tristanian among the crew. An interesting and
resourceful man, as I expect you will discover."

Heat haze and Sahara Desert dust enveloped the ship when I first
spoke with Julian Swain a couple of days out of Tenerife. He is a tall,
slim, dark-bearded, curly-haired Adonis with a vibrant gleam in his
eyes. It is said that, at 30, Tristan girls have ceased to interest him.
He looked at me with the suspicious slanted hooded gaze that
Tristanians reserve for inquisitive strangers who seek to pry into their
affairs. Then he began to relax.

"Pitcairn. You know Pitcairn?"

"Yes."

"You been there?"

"Yes."

"Our children back home write to those Pitcairn children. Takes
'bout four months for a letter. They compare notes loike. How it is
on each island and that. Our school teacher is now Tristanian. Only
the Admin and Doctor from outside. It's best that way. That way we
all know what goin' on, loike."

Julian Swain is a man of resource and character. In 1980 a *Royal
Viking* ship was scheduled to call at Tristan, weather permitting, in
the course of a world cruise. On the spur of the moment, he sent a
telegram from Tristan to the ship asking if there was a vacancy
among the crew. There was; he was told to be ready; and he had been

XII - THE SWEARING IN OF THE ISLAND'S JUDGE

XIII - Longwood House

XIV - High Knoll Fort

XV - SANDY BAY CHAPEL

XVI - School Sports Day on New Year's Day

XVII - Smiling faces on School Sports Day

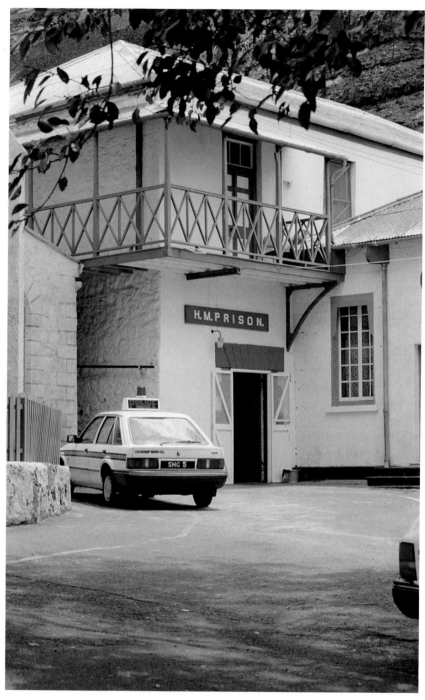

XVIII - The Island's Gaol

XIX - John Musk's General Store - Jamestown

XX - The Potato patches on Tristan da Cunha

XXI - TRISTAN'S STONE HOUSES

XXII - SEALS OFF TRISTAN DA CUNHA

XXIII - Sailing Long Boats on Tristan da Cunha

at sea ever since. Not all the time with *Royal Viking*. He transferred to the old *RMS* for the Falklands war and had been with Curnow until now. He was on his last voyage with the company and the new ship. Or so he said.

"Sometimes I go out with friends, but I don' feel roight loike. I feel I want to go home - go out and catch a sheep or sail to Nightingale. Then I think of those South African girls. They are noice and polite loike. They don' answer you back."

Julian was on duty at the gangway when I went ashore at St. Helena.

"You seen the new Admin yet?" Staccato, straight.

I hesitated. "Ah yes. The new Administrator. Yes I have."

"Quiet loike. Maybe he be OK."

"Yes. Hopefully. No doubt everyone on Tristan will wait and see. Have you heard what is going on in the outside world lately?"

"No, sir. I ain't heard nuttin'."

"Nor have I. For all we know, Margaret Thatcher may have gone into a nunnery."

He laughed rich and deep. "That be askin' a bit much."

"So you are signing off in Cape Town after the Tristan call? Another period of your life comes to an end."

"Yes, sir. That's it. I hope I make it. The girls'll help. I'm stayin' with my sister. She got lots o' friends. I loikes them South African girls."

And I thought, as I clambered down the gangway clutching my cassette case of precious music tapes, them South African girls will undoubtedly loike you too.

CHAPTER 23

Tristan Da Cunha:
An Island on Its Own Terms

'You can be a poor man on Tristan
And still be rich' - Willie Repetto
who led the return to the island in
1963.

From St. Helena, the *RMS* set course south to Tristan da Cunha
and the Roaring Forties. Two days out from landfall, the mid-
morning ocean was an oily calm at 32° south, the sky a brilliant blue
and cloudless apart from an ominous line of grey ahead with patches
of dark towering cumulus. All change perhaps, sudden and sharp, if
the frontal wall did not disperse.

Julian Swain had been painting the deck and bulwarks. "Got to
smarten the ship up for Tristan," he said. "Otherwise the people
blame me." A broad grin. There was a blue and white handkerchief
band round his forehead. His black curly locks fell loose below his
collar. A gold locket flapped against his neck from a black chain. His
beard looked deeper and darker, his eyes sharper. He was wearing
a blue singlet and grey tight-fitting denim trousers. In his belt, a knife
completed a carefully chosen homecoming ensemble. Those girls in
South Africa were going to be worked hard.

"Well, Julian. You are nearly home."

"Yes, sir. An' 'bout toime too. I'll be up after a sheep tomorrow."

* * *

I wasn't going to write about Tristan at all. I don't quite know why.
Perhaps I was feeling lazy as we came closer to arrival. Perhaps I
was preoccupied with St. Helena and did not want to be diverted.

Perhaps it was the islanders' well-known dislike of idle questions, prying eyes and journalistic instant judgements. Perhaps, even now, it would be prudent not to make the attempt. But Tristan creeps up on you, poses so many questions, gives so few answers. And even when it does, it seems only with such reluctance and wary circumspection that you cannot be sure that you have probed to the heart. Indeed how could you - in two days with so singular an island people? Inevitably you are left pondering the superficial and the impressionistic.

The *RMS* was about to make its maiden call at Tristan da Cunha. Its scheduled diversion from the St. Helena to Cape Town sector occurs once a year only. This was the compelling attraction - indeed the focus - of the entire voyage for some of the passengers, not least the World's Most Travelled Couple. They were so steamed up about the unpredictability of the weather and thus of getting ashore at Tristan that they could think and talk about virtually nothing else. It consumed their minds and conversation. True, they ordered Castle lager for themselves alone each day, at lunch; and rosé wine for themselves alone each day, at dinner. This was at Wellington House, otherwise known as Yon's Café in Jamestown, where they stayed while the *RMS* did the St. Helena/Ascension/St. Helena shuttle. For them, St. Helena - previously visited and crossed off the list - was a time-wasting interlude that had to be endured while they ticked away the days on the calendar.

Disclaimers abounded - not unlike the one I had in a letter from ODA when I first went to St. Helena as Budgetary Aid Adviser in 1985:

While every effort is made to ensure that the information and advice given in this letter and the accompanying documentation are accurate, this Administration cannot accept any responsibility for the accuracy of any such information or advice, or for the consequences of any action taken in reliance upon it.

To which the wary recipient, about to embark upon an ODA

sponsored overseas assignment, can surely reply: Why not?

The W.M.T.C. read and re-read, dissected and debated the St. Helena Shipping Company's warning to passengers about the hazards and uncertainties of getting ashore at Tristan - and getting back on board again:-

LANDING AT TRISTAN DA CUNHA

Because of the sudden weather changes which are a feature of the Tristan area, landings from the anchorage off Edinburgh are permitted only at the Master's discretion and under his set conditions. Such terms are concerned solely with the safety of passengers and are designed to cover both disembarkation and re-embarkation.

Passengers who are able to negotiate vertical rope ladders and who are aged between 10 and 70 years can be considered for shore visits (subject to Masters' approval), but persons outside these age limits or who are not considered to have sufficient mobility for the landing procedure are most unlikely to be able to go ashore.

Passengers are also required to produce a valid medical insurance when requesting permission to go ashore.

You might have thought all that was quite enough. But the Government of Tristan da Cunha had one too, albeit considerably shorter:

NOTICE

All passengers disembarking at Tristan da Cunha do so at their own risk. The Government of Tristan da Cunha, its servants and agents, will not accept any responsibility or liability for any loss or personal injury, howsoever arising, sustained by any passenger disembarking at Tristan da Cunha, whether such loss or injury shall be sustained in the course of disembarkation or re-embarkation, while travelling to or from the shore or while on shore.

Received a copy of the above notice this 12th day of January, 1992 ...

More dire forebodings and documentation were to come. Indeed, every passenger had to sign a 700-word four-page indemnity releasing the company, the ship, the administration of Tristan da Cunha and everyone in the landing barges for any kind of involvement in anything remotely connected with disembarkation or returning to the ship.

So would the W.M.T.C. get their feet on the soil of Tristan da Cunha or not? If they could not - did not - land what then? Would they be judged as having 'been' to Tristan? "What is your definition," they asked, "of whether you have visited a country? We have to know for the purpose of our report. By sea, that is. Never mind transit lounges at 3 a.m. What happens if no-one gets ashore? Have we been there or not? Will we satisfy the club rules? The Travellers' Century Club of Los Angeles is very prestigious you know, and very careful about recognising a visit ..."

Why should I have to help solve this self-indulgent, self-inflicted problem? Ask your bloody club for Pete's sake! ... That's what I wanted to say ...

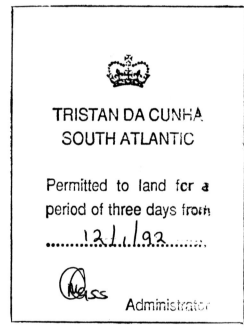

Oh well, I thought, here goes." If a vessel is given clearance and comes into a port of entry anchorage or dock, it will thus have entered the country concerned and become subject to its laws and requirements. Then all on board will *de facto* have entered it too, irrespective of whether or not their feet touch the soil of the promised land. So if the ship's engine stops, the anchor is lowered, but you can't go ashore at Tristan even though your passport has been stamped with permission to land and you have paid the £3 landing fee, then I suppose ..."

"We like that. We like that," they said as if at the gates of a new Jerusalem. "So it could be 305 countries after all, even if we don't get ashore. And we'll still be the World's Most Travelled Couple of the Travellers' Century Club of Los Angeles. That's a relief."

In the event, they did get ashore, passports duly stamped. They walked around for an hour or so with infinite disdain and returned to the ship, statistical mission accomplished. In this case it was **not** better to travel than to arrive. But both were the product of cut price travel and ego and, in the end, worthless. To me anyway; not, of course, to them, to their fellow club members, or they hoped, to the *Guinness Book of Records*. They eyed its editor, Norris McWhirter, across the dining saloon of the *RMS* with the predatory instincts of the piranha.

The voyage over, their home in Long Island, New York, would claim them for a week or two before they set off again - in search of that passport entry for the British Indian Ocean Territory and all its non-existent indigènes. That would leave only Midway, Afghanistan and Iraq for them to clock up the total of 309 'countries' listed by their club for its Wandering Albatross members.

The omens for landing had, in fact, not been good. A day out of Tristan, the *RMS* sailed on through tranquil seas under a cloudless sky - except for that line of black cloud still pierced by thunderous towering cumulus right ahead. For three days before arrival, the boats could not be launched, the port could not be worked. A small Danish freighter, the *Arctis Carrier*, chartered by the British Government, had been waiting to discharge its cargo of cement, cement mixers and tractors from South Africa for a much needed port sea wall extension. No boat could get out to it. Not surprisingly: there are only about sixty days scattered throughout the year when working the port is possible.

It seemed that the *RMS* brought the good weather with it. The ship dropped anchor at 10 a.m. on 12th January, 1992 and lowered a gangway. Nothing special about that, you might think: You would be wrong. "You can come here for years and not experience weather like this" said Colin Dellar. "We have never before been able to lower a ship's gangway. It's always been a rope ladder over the side."

Landing barges ferried cargo and passengers ashore every hour or so. The design of the barges is functional and simple. There are no frills and no aids to inagility. The barge rises four feet in the swell, bashes against the lower platform of the gangway and falls away fast. There is a split-second timing of the moment when barge gunwale and gangway meet for your hesitant step off the ship. The gunwale surround is only a foot wide; then a drop of about four feet down to the flat bottom. There will be a hand or two for the geriatric and the brittle-boned; but no fixture or railing to grasp as you leap. One barge had three portable steps down from the stern; OK if you could negotiate the loose rope knotted to the gangway, a swinging tiller and the 'captain of boats' in order to get on to them. So take off and pray you don't dislocate, break or twist something. If you do, it is made abundantly clear that it is nobody's fault but your own.

The barge rides the rollers on the way in and awaits the lull between a series before the signal comes from the prow. Then with the engine at full throttle, you surge in between two arms of 'dollase' sea defences, a sharp right turn into the tiny harbour and crash bang against a solid concrete wall, six feet or so below the wharf deck. There is a steel ladder set rigid and sheer, its narrow steps inches only away from the wall. Leap at the right moment, hang on as the barge falls away, scramble up, ungainly and clumsy before your bottom foot gets smashed with the next swell. I was pulled safely up and over by Norris McWhirter on the first occasion. He was doing a running service; perhaps a first for an editor of the *Guinness Book*.

Along the seawall by the boats sat thirty or more men in identical blue denim overalls, showing no signs of interest in the faltering landfalls of the passengers from the *RMS* or what happened to them thereafter.

No sign says WELCOME TO TRISTAN DA CUNHA. No representative of government or company is at the landing. No one pays any attention; no one speaks. You see the path up the hill and take it. More men sitting, looking out to sea, backs to the path. They do not turn to look as you pass. Women likewise, scarves round their heads, expressionless. The men's faces are striking: sun browned, lantern-jawed, strong, impassive, eyes deep set and penetrating, some heavily lined, character in every wrinkle. Lives pitted against the sea where ocean is always master. A maiden voyage of a new ship to Tristan was - just a ship, it seemed. And then, well, not much. Even with the island's governor on board.

Not so the children. In the afternoon they chattered and chirped and scrambled over everything, eyeing the fine main lounge, the sun deck, the technical marvels on the bridge and the goodies in the gift shop. Children are children, until the maturing process changes and hardens in the mixture of the inherited and the environmental.

"To visit Tristan da Cunha is to visit another world, another life, another time," says the Curnow brochure. How right it is. It is a close run thing as to whether Pitcairn Island, midway between New Zealand and the Panama Canal or Tristan da Cunha is the most isolated island to fly the Union Flag. Norris McWhirter had correctly described Tristan as the remotest inhabited island, being 1,315 miles from St. Helena. Pitcairn has the southernmost island of French Polynesia somewhat closer to the north.

Tristan da Cunha, discovered by the Portuguese navigator in 1506, owes its existence as a settlement to Napoleon Bonaparte: more specifically to the exile of the Emperor to St. Helena in 1815. Tristan was annexed by Britain in 1816 and a small garrison set up to forestall any attempt by the French to use the island as a base for rescuing the defeated general. When the garrison was withdrawn, one man, a corporal, elected to stay on. His gravestone in white marble - the only one in that colour - is still tended today by his descendants:

WILLIAM GLASS
Born at Kelso Scotland
the founder of
this settlement of
Tristan da Cunha
in which he resided 37 years
and fell asleep in Jesus
Nov. 24 1853
Aged 67 years

Glass, Repetto, Swain, Green, Rogers, Hagan, Lavarello: until recently those were the only seven family names in use on Tristan. Now there is an eighth - Patterson - an Englishman married to a Tristanian. Sailor sons all - English from Nelson's fleet, Americans from New Bedford, Italian, Dutch, mixed racial strains from St. Helena and South Africa. Tall, rangey and nimble-footed, the skills of the men against the fury of the sea are matched only by the Pitcairners. The two islands exchange newsletters and, as Julian Swain had told me, the children have corresponded from time to time. A four month journey for a letter is commonplace. There is, however, another lesser known instant link between the two most remotely populated islands in the world. Andy Repetto, Radio Officer on Tristan da Cunha, and Tom Christian, Radio Officer on Pitcairn, now have a trans-oceanic amateur wireless sked. For ham radio eavesdroppers, it must be the most sought after conversation there is.

It is twenty-four miles round the roughly circular coast of Tristan da Cunha and about eight miles across. At 38° latitude south, it is just north of the roaring forties. Five thousand miles from Britain and 1,519 miles to Cape Town, less to St. Helena where its Governor resides. There is a resident Administrator who changed with our visit. The new one had come from a posting in the Bahamas. "Going to be different" he said with undeniable accuracy. He had brought a new Metro, a tax-free export, freight paid by the FCO. With about six miles of road on the island, I reckoned that it might come to rate entry in the *Guinness Book of Records* as the motor car that had travelled the longest distance with the lowest recorded mileage. If that matters.

A helpful piece of paper is handed to you as your passport is stamped. You now recognise that it, like everything else you have received, contains the customary disclaimer at the end:

GOVERNMENT OF TRISTAN DA CUNHA

Welcome to Tristan da Cunha.

We hope that the weather will be kind and that you will be able to come ashore ..

Visitors will be brought into the small harbour by launch or barge. The road winds up from the harbour to a T junction at the Museum and Handicraft shop. Take the left fork to walk into the village passing the Vicar's house and The Residency on your right and St. Mary's School on your left. At the next intersection you will find Jane's Café and Swimming Pool on your right with the Prince Philip Hall and The Pub in front of you. The swimming pool is closed in the winter; the Café will be open during the day when a Ship is in port; The Pub is open on weekdays from 6 p.m. to 9 p.m. and closed on Sundays.

A further walk towards the mountain along the path behind The Hall will bring you to St. Mary's Church. The island enjoys a Royal tradition with the Church harmonium. The first was presented by Queen Mary in the early 1930s; the second one in 1960 and the present one in 1989 were both presented by Queen Elizabeth the Second.

St. Joseph's Roman Catholic Church, stands in a clearing just below the entrance to Jane's Café.

An alternate route at the Museum T junction is to turn right and walk past the Island Store on your left towards the Administration Offices. Up the steps into the main building and to the left is a short corridor to the Treasury where Travellers Cheques in US dollars and SA Rand may be cashed and notes exchanged for Sterling. The Post Office is on the right of the building with an entrance on the seaward side. Stamps, First Day Covers and Postcards are on sale.

Uphill from the Post Office is the road to the hospital and, two miles away, the Potato Patches. Downhill from the Post Office is the crayfish processing factory overlooking the harbour ... Follow the signposts and do not disturb the cows that graze freely in the village.

Finally, a word of warning. The Government of Tristan da Cunha accept no responsibility for any injury sustained by a visitor while ashore or being conveyed between ship and shore.

There is another sort of warning that could, I suppose, be given. Tristan da Cunha does not rejoice in the luxury of instant direct dial international telephone calls by satellite. With neither fax nor telex, in 1992 it still talked to the outside world by W/T outmoded morsecode. R/T to ships only. Secret and Top Secret communications, if any, from the FCO to the Administrator arrived in enciphered morse and had to be deciphered through the laborious antequated process of what are called 'one time pads'.

I went to the island store and saw this:

PUBLIC NOTICE
Site Board and Planning Committee
Mr. Trevor Glass has applied for permission to build a clothes line in accordance with the attached plan. Any objections to be lodged with the Chief Islander before 26 December, 1991.

Distribution:Chairman SB and PC
All Notice Boards
The Pub
The Café

An elaborate plan of the proposed domestic clothes line and the neighbouring plots and houses was attached.

There was a second notice below:

TRISTAN DA CUNHA
WOOD CUTTING FOR PENSIONERS

In accordance with the decision of the Island Council, pensioners who have fireplaces or open fires may cut living wood for half a day per alternative year, the next occasion being January, 1992.

If a pensioner cuts wood himself he may do so for four hours. If he has someone to do it for him, he may have two hours.

Names of the cutters, the date for cutting and the area chosen for cutting must be given in advance to the Chief Islander.
13 December, 1991
c.c. Chief Islander
      Agricultural Officer

"I hope you are not going to print that." It was a woman's voice in the island store as I wrote down the texts of the notices. It was a polite question or request that I was to hear again, a reflection of the islanders' suspicion of strangers who put them under passing inspection and go off to denigrate them in newspaper, book or film. That, anyway, is what the Tristanians think.

Nurse Repetto is open, fresh and pretty. She had become an SRN at Cardiff; but was soon to return, this time to Glasgow, to do midwifery - and to get married to a Scotsman. I asked her what she perceived as the essential difference between Tristanian and Saint. "Are you going to print it?" she asked, giving me no answer as island caution and reticence surfaced. "So many people come here and stay a fortnight and think they understand everything and go away and write a book and it's all rubbish. Lies."

"What is?"

"What they say: except for Allan Crawford's *Tristan da Cunha and the Roaring Forties*. He got a few facts wrong, but on the whole it is the best." Allan Crawford first landed on Tristan in 1937. He too was apparently met without curiosity.   "After all, You's an h'Englishman same as we all is."

The admirable chef on the *RMS* was David Stroud, a Saint paying his first visit to Tristan.   How did he perceive his remote fellow islanders?   "I walked among the houses," he said.   "I wanted to get to know them a little.   I would briefly see a face through the window, then the curtains would be drawn.   They seem to be the most uncurious of people."   How right.   Curiosity breaks the barriers of self-sufficiency.

I climbed ponderously up to the top of the 1961 volcano which sits below the main mountain to the left of the settlement.   Well, not quite to the top.   The rocks became too sharp and broken when I gave up - perhaps because I was in the wrong clothes and not wearing my Samoan *lavalava*.   A few puffs of steam came through the deep fissures.   The rocks were warm.   I was glad that it was one of Tristan's precious fine days with little wind.

I went back down towards the little harbour with a sense of having intruded, like entering someone's home, an uninvited guest.   'A bit eerie' was the judgement of one seasoned woman globetrotter.

At the landing, I stood with Second Purser Angie Read until all the other passengers had gingerly negotiated the jump down to the surging and swaying gunwale of the barge.   The sea had risen. Rollers pursued each other through the narrow entrance.   A woman passenger jumped too late, slipped, fell and was clawed back by one man; an instant Tristan response.   A shoe fell into the water.   The paper warnings made sudden sense.   Then as the boat dropped momentarily away from the stone wall, a second boatman leaned over, head down, arm outstretched.   His hand found the shoe as the boat surged back to the wall.   He scooped up the shoe, head and arm shot up above the gunwale to split-second safety as the boat crashed against the wall.   There was no more than an inch to spare on either side of his head.   It would have been crushed into oblivion like an eggshell ...

Angie went white, then red, white again and was, I think, nearly sick. My mouth hung open, immobilised. No one else had seen it. Our eyes met. The boatmen were laughing at some joke. We were not. She came to my cabin. A neat whisky was of some help, gradually.

One boatman was Darren Repetto. The other's nickname was 'Doc.' The usual Tristanian reticence prevailed. That was all we could discover at the time - in 'the Land of the Blue Men,' as the outgoing Administrator Bernard Pauncefort had whimsically described the effect of the uniform PWD issue overalls worn by the islanders who worked the port and the boats.

A few days later, I recounted what we had seen to Julian Swain. He was not surprised. "That's Tristan," he said. "We do that, loike, every day. No fuss. No big t'ing."

"And Doc's name?"

"Colin Hagan. He's a mate o' mine. But we'd all do that." And, I thought, it was all for a shoe.

*   *   *

I went ashore again next morning, the gangway down, the sea gratifyingly quiescent. I waited with a crew member, a Saint, for the landing barge.

"I got a luttle boy of sux over there" he said suddenly.

"Where?"

"Over there. On Tristan."

"You have?"

"Yes. I's goin' to see him now."

"Where is he?"

"On shore. Over there in the Settlement." He pointed vaguely.

"Does he know you are coming?"

"I guess so. Maybe his mummy tell him."

"Have you any others?"

"Oh yes."

"Where?"

"On St. Helena."

"How many?"

"Two."

"What then would you say is the difference between the women of St. Helena and the women of Tristan?" He looked reflective.

"That's a hard one. I can't say. That's a hard one."

"Yes" I said, "I guess it was."

"When do you sign off?"

"After the shuttle from Ascension."

"What are you going to do at home?"

"Make some more babies I suppose." He chuckled with anticipatory relish ...

In the window of the island store was a new notice:

THERE WILL BE A DANCE

TONIGHT (13 JAN) FOR JULIAN

FROM 9 - 12 p.m.

Everyone welcome

There will be no tea break

Next day Julian Swain would be gone again on the *RMS*, off to South Africa and his new life. The people of Tristan da Cunha would gather to say goodbye and to wish him well. But what did the absence of a 'tea break' mean?

"Simple," they said when I asked. "Midway through the dance everyone goes home, has tea and comes back again. Saves catering problems - especially since it is not always tea that features in the domestic tea break."

Alongside the Administrator's house half a dozen Tristan long-boats were lashed down in series on the path. Lighter than the sturdy Pitcairn long boats, the Tristan craft have been adapted for launching and landing through the surf on exposed beaches. Each boat consists, surprisingly it seemed, of one thickness of canvas over a light wooden frame. The average length is twenty- six feet, with a beam of six and a half feet. A mainsail and a jib are carried, the mast being nineteen feet high.

Today, fishing is the principal source of revenue and employment. The famous and delectable Tristan crayfish or rock lobster is caught in semi-cylindrical mesh-covered traps about a metre long. The traps are buoyed and hauled to the surface about three times a day, the fishing nets up to six times depending on the time available, currents and catches.

When conditions are judged to be suitable, a fishing day is called by the beating of an iron gong hanging in the open in the middle of the Settlement. The average number of such days in the year is only about sixty. A more than good daily catch of crayfish for two men working a boat is about 2,000 lbs. in high season.

The first canning factory was built in 1949. The entire building and site now lies beneath the lava of the 1961 eruption. After the return of the islanders in 1963, the South Atlantic Islands Development Corporation (registered in Bermuda) renegotiated its exclusive concession for the dependency's marine resources in coastal waters and built a new factory overlooking the harbour landing. About every two months, a fishing vessel comes in from Cape Town and from the high seas for the cooking, canning and shipment of its catch.

So it is perhaps that with a per capita annual income tax of less than a pound - I'll read that again - a thriving fishing and canning industry and, as with St. Helena, a good philatelic reputation, the island of Tristan da Cunha pays its way without recourse, unlike St. Helena, to the British taxpayer. There is a rugged independence and confident self-sufficiency in the people of Tristan that seems quite different from the softer more open and gentler people of St. Helena. The key to the difference is clearly the climate: that of Tristan is harsh, demanding, mainly relentless and cold. It is a courageous community surviving almost entirely by its own efforts. It asks no favours and expects to be accepted on its own terms: the terms of a people who live side by side in one area only of their island with houses and buildings of such cleanliness and white-washed old-world charm as to be almost unreal in an environmentally polluted world. For the Tristanians, oceanic isolation is their protection from the prying eyes and intrusions of the 'h' outside.' It is not for nothing that the settlement is named Edinburgh of the Seven Seas.

Bernard Pauncefort again: "It is, I think, the only island community where the people live a successful mixture of a cash and subsistence economy. The sea gives them both, of course. If they want something they will work together to earn the money for it. When they want to go to the potato patches or when the weather is right to go to Nightingale, they will do so."

"And the relationship between the Administrator and the Chief Islander?"

"It is a loosely defined thing. There is no job description for the elected post of Chief Islander. We meet regularly, of course, to discuss the problems he brings to me. And there is an Island Council, elected on behalf of the community of just under three hundred islanders. The job of the Administrator, in my view, is to interfere as little as he can."

I was reminded of an old South Pacific story. In the now distant days of the Gilbert and Ellice Islands Colony, a new High Commissioner for the Western Pacific stepped ashore on a remote atoll to be greeted by the resident Gilbertese district officer. Tour of island and people accomplished, the High Commissioner turned to this official and asked:

"And tell me, do the people pay their taxes?"

"Of course, sir. It is my job to see that they do."

"I know. I know. But what does the government do in return for the taxes that the people pay?"

A smile lightened the face of the district officer.

"We leave them alone sir."

I had a feeling that there had been more than a little bit of that, thirty years on, from the departing Administrator of Tristan da Cunha.

The police force of Tristan has an establishment of one: a police constable, supported by two part-timers. In the past, the rôle of the solitary officer of the law was largely ceremonial. Not any more, it would seem. There have been a number of alcohol-related burglaries and thefts in recent years; but no charges and thus no convictions.

It is notoriously difficult in small island communities where families are so linked and inter-dependent to obtain witnesses prepared to testify in court to establish proof of guilt. Everyone will know - or soon know- the perpetrators, but none will be prepared to come forward. Family relationships are complex and historically attuned in matters of status, perceived preferment and influence. In an apparently stable community, deep-seated rivalries and antagonisms lie dormant until there is an act so outrageous as to provoke a breach of silence. Then anger will prevail over reticence as families may be split beyond repair. Such schisms go deep and they endure. Only then will there be an overriding motivation for reporting crime and providing the evidence for prosecution. Even on Tristan, life and the ethics of society do not stay unchanged.

Another example is sport. Governor Alan Hoole had noted the contrast with St. Helena. "There is no organised sport on Tristan any more such as football, rugby, tennis or hockey. Only the children play and swim in the pool in the summer. All that remains is darts and snooker. This is in total contrast to St. Helena where, for many, the whole of life is devoted to finishing work and getting out in the evening to play skittles, tennis, cricket or football. And shooting remains a favoured competitive sport in St. Helena."

I was browsing through the exemplary and surprising Museum and Craft Centre. There was an old mail bag in leather which looked like a Berber water bottle from the mountains of Morocco. Attached to it was a brass plate, optimistically inscribed

To Officer in Charge
Department of Transport
TRISTAN DA CUNHA

Then a female voice:

"Peter, I'm just going to buy a penguin."

"What do you want a penguin for?"

"Because I feel like it."

The independent spirit of Tristan da Cunha was catching on, it seemed, among the passengers of the *RMS*.

The *RMS* weighed anchor at 2 p.m. on Tuesday, 14th January, 1992. Just before, the recently elected Chief Islander, Lewis Glass and his wife, left the ship after lunching on board with Governor Hoole and Delia. He jumped easily on to the barge, three long practised strides along the gunwale and down. Laughter all round - not least from Julian Swain who was watching all this from the forward deck. Cheers, salutes, waves, wide grins, reticence and inhibition gone, as the Tristanians bad farewell to their departing son and brother. Three long blasts of goodbye and the ship moved off round the island before setting course due east for Cape Town. It was a gently swelling ocean with a warming sun, a light breeze and fair weather cumulus encircling the horizon. The ship was rock-steady, vibration-less. The red ensign flapped gently at the stern jackstaff. Oceanic perfection in peace. The Mediterranean at its best you might conclude, except for a single albatross gliding gracefully above the wake behind the ship.

The island of Tristan da Cunha was slipping away west, enveloped in cloud, just as its peak and all above the great plateau had been since our arrival. Were we to be deprived?

Two hours and thirty miles out, there was an unexpected change. For no perceivable reason, the cloud cover parted like the curtains of a great theatre stage. The 7,690 foot summit emerged resplendent, for the first time during our visit. On both sides, the land slipped gracefully and gently away until, left and right, it plunged sharply and steeply into the ocean.

"Symmetry in silhouette," I said to a young wife, struggling with a new set of camera filters. "Corny, I suppose?" "Yes" she said, as she chose a filter. Not so, I told myself. That is exactly what it is, the sun behind the island in the west. Symmetry in silhouette.

The splendour lasted for less than twenty minutes. Then the curtain of cloud closed in again. The peak and the island of Tristan da Cunha were gone. A maiden voyage was done.

*   *   *

On night two out of Tristan and seven hundred miles east bound for Cape Town, the sun was sinking through patches of fair weather cumulus into a welcoming sea. An albatross had stayed with the ship: whirling, wheeling, gliding, circling, wings bending little to take the wind, a glorious ballet of flight astern. Then for the royal fly-past, the bird would come gently in towards the ship as if to land, cruise ten feet above and always to the starboard of the sun deck, never reaching abreast of the bridge, then wheel away in a great serene arc.

It would cross and re-cross the wake of the ship, mile after mile behind, skimming the broken sea side on, wing tip seemingly within inches, but never touching the restless waves: until it returned, head down, eyes on the deck, an eight foot wing span, for another aerial inspection of the ship, then away again. I watched the albatross for an hour, wondering whether the Red Arrows had learned from it, glorying in the sovereign beauty of its flight, and pondering like those at sea in these waters throughout the centuries, how and why and for how long and how far.

Suddenly there were three albatross where before there had been but one. And a tiny 'wideawake' pitched up ten feet from my head, looked down quizzically and was off, little wings flapping energetically, making hard work, it seemed, of the wind currents and the chase. In the cabin, I put on a tape of the Orpheus Chamber Orchestra playing Haydn's Symphony No. 77. Loud. The polished beauty of the playing and the silken gentility of the music of the first movement somehow seemed right. I wondered why no composer had written an Albatross Symphony: perhaps because it would have had to be the most graceful of all.

Next morning, the skies were empty. The albatross had gone, back home perhaps to Tristan in the wake of a fishing boat which passed in the night on course for the island. I resented that it might do so when I could not. This time I put on headphones and listened to the Beaux Arts Trio playing Beethoven's Archduke Trio. Somehow it helped to erase and at the same time to enhance the memory of a regal albatross and the land and the people of Tristan da Cunha.

CHAPTER 24

A South Pacific Tristan Da Cunha

As the shadow of Napoleon Bonaparte is still inescapably with St. Helena, so that of the awesome volcanic eruption of 1961 and the enforced evacuation which followed it, is with the older people of Tristan da Cunha - over thirty years on. It was a crucial part of the formative life of the present Chief Islander who was a teenage lad, he says, when it all happened.

The story has been documented by others. Told and retold. It is thus well-known - available anyway - to the world. How then to bring alive its awesomeness and horror to the new generation of Tristanians who know of it only through the stories of their parents and grand-parents? Surely there can be nothing worthwhile to add now to the sum of their recollections - not least because human memory is ultimately kind and the patience of the young with the past is limited.

Why not, I thought, search for a comparable cataclysm in another small isolated island and, by so doing, relate the two. A common heritage of suffering is mutually strengthening. Pain shared is pain understood and thus relieved. So I looked into the past - part of my own past, as it happens. There I found a South Pacific Tristan da Cunha in the Polynesian Kingdom of Tonga. So here is its story to place beside that of the Tristan of 1961 - for those who suffered in Tristan to ponder and those in Tonga to share.

Away to the north-west of Ha'apai and 400 miles from Nuku'alofa lies Niuafo'ou, the most remote island to fly the red cross of the Tongan flag. You might know of it as Tin Can Island. You get a glimpse of it as you sail on the fringe of Tongan waters from Samoa to Fiji. A stark and lonely island, it is, like Pitcairn, a maritime whistle-stop.

The heart of it lies in the nature of the island itself and its active volcanic history. The summit of the central crater is about 600 feet above sea level. The top of what is now the central cone blew off many centuries ago. It is filled by a large lake fed by hot springs. The size of Niuafo'ou is officially put at nineteen square miles: of these the lake accounts for six. The rest of the island is a near-circular crust of fertile land encircling the main crater. From the air, it resembles a large doughnut. Locked within the high volcanic rim is a series of small craters and crater lakes. Within the lakes are more volcanic upthrusts, within which in turn are yet more lakes. There are lakes within volcanoes within lakes within volcanoes within lakes within one huge island volcano. There are more than thirty points of volcanic eruption; and life for the people of Niuafo'ou has been one of destroyed villages, ruined crops and loss of life and property. It may seem strange that the island remained inhabited; but the deep-rooted sentimental attachment of the Polynesian to his own tribal or family land is the reason.

One inky night in August 1886, an earthquake shook the island with a gentle swaying motion. Smaller shocks followed. Then with a tremendous roar, a volcanic eruption mushroomed up 3,000 feet above the lake and the earthquake ceased. A violent thunderstorm followed and lightning struck in many places. A blizzard of black dust and sand weighed down the houses and vegetation. Spasmodic eruptions like geysers occurred during the next eighteen days and clouds of dust dimmed the light of day. In July 1929, there was another nightmare of erupting violence which destroyed the village of Futu. The people were awakened by a low rumbling as fire broke out on the hillside to the south-east. The aged, the sick and young children were evacuated to the high ground of the island's circular ridge. From three vents in a fracture that opened in the crust of the earth, molten rock descended on Futu. Soon the abandoned buildings had been consumed by fire and buried under floods of heavy basaltic lava. Pouring into the ocean, the hot flows killed fish, sent up clouds of steam and heaped mountains of black sand on the rocky coast.

In 1935 and 1936, the violence returned again. Ahau, the most fertile part of the island, was destroyed, the village of Petani threatened. In 1943, another eruption wrecked houses and ruined food crops. Then, three years later, came the great ordeal of the people of Niuafo'ou when their island was all but submerged by the savage onslaught which struck it.

The day's work was over and it was night. The hurricane lamps shone in the faces of the men of Angaha as they sat drinking *kava*. Stone cracked on stone as the girl crushed the dry root for the next mixing. It was the timeless custom of this village and every village; the nightly gossip of the *faikava*, the scandals and speculations of tongues relaxed by the ceremonial brown liquid. Old men, withered in body but yet fresh in mind, basked in the reflective talk of their age; while the young listened and learned of love and sport and how to win in both.

A warm, friendly evening at seven o'clock on the night of 9th September, 1946 - like many another before and since.

From the distance, faintly, came a rumble as of thunder. Ears lifted to the west whence the sound had come. Abruptly the chatter was stilled. Inside was silence but for the lamps which hissed as they swung back and forth from the hooks on the beam. A chill ripple ran through the hut. *Kava* swilled over the broad lip of the wooden bowl.

Throughout the night, Niuafo'ou shivered and creaked, giving to all that claustrophobic fear for life and property peculiar to earthquakes and hurricanes. The dawn came bleak and comfortless. Over the island's smouldering ruin hung a film of steam pierced here and there by spirals of blue smoke from lava fires which still burned in the undergrowth. The island itself was a scarred and battered shell; and the principal town of Angaha had all but vanished.

Wireless telegraphy had been installed on Niuafo'ou in 1930. The operator in 1946 was S.M. Manu, who had the presence of mind to keep a diary of the terrible events which then took place.

These are some extracts from what he wrote:

9.9.46: 8.15 p.m. Copra Inspector called from verandah that something queer is seen. Ran out and to my horror the western approach to Angaha is all in flames and smoke thousands of feet high. Can hear clearly big trees and coconut trees snap when waves of lava reach them. My estimate as well as others, was that the fire is now at the end of Angaha - almost at the hospital. Abandoned everything and started for the hill. Fire seems to cover all western approaches from the sea up to village of Esia, so ran towards Sapa'ata village. Joined by teacher outside the station. We started at a slow trot, hoping that the fire will not reach the town. Stopped near end of Angaha and had another look at the eruption. A big flash of lightning ran from the sea from a north-easterly direction to about 100 yards from where we stood accompanied by an eruption from the sea, directly in front of Dougal Quensell's property. We now ran for our lives. When we reached Sapa'ata, the fire looked as if it is where we stood not three minutes ago. People running to the hill, a whole mass of men, women, children and animals, all struggling together. Whole place brightly lit by fire. Moon obscured by fire and smoke. Piu was considered unsafe as it was too close to Angaha, so all run up to Mokotu point, about a mile from Angaha. Could see from Mokotu fire raging at Angaha. Wireless masts still stand in midst of fire. After about an hour, we went to Piu where we saw the destruction of the wireless station, Government offices and quarters by two craters, one about ten yards from our kitchen and one beside Fotofili's house about twenty yards from the office. There are other small openings at various places at Angaha which spout fire but not lava.

11 p.m. Light rain mixed with sand came down. For the first time I realised that I have nothing except the shirt and *vala* which I wore, my only things saved together with office and safe keys and tuning fork. Other things lost. Later found out that I shared this misfortune with Magistrate, Police officers, Assistant Operator Robert Tupou, Copra Inspector, storekeeper and others. People now start building shelters. Back from Piu, wet, found no place to sleep so went down to Fata'ulua village and spent an uncomfortable night at the house of Ha'angana's father-in-law.

10.9.46: 10 a.m. In addition to three craters at Angaha, about nine others are found from 'Utu Palapu to 'Alalea, the crater at the outskirts of Angaha, about a hundred yards from dispensary. All these craters are in line along the beach to the dispensary. Pule erupted in the sea, and runs in a westerly direction, covering the landing place and stopping. There is an opening of about twenty or thirty yards between them. Lava has extended right out to sea; whether it will stay or not will depend on the durability of the lava to stand the force of the waves. The new beach is covered by a kind of rough black sand, and boats can now land there with ease.

11.9.46: 11.30 a.m. About 11 a.m. we managed to pull out the small safe
from Government office. We broke this safe and recovered £34 in silver.
All paper currency burned. Unable to pull out the big safe as it was
surrounded by hot thick lava and covered by hot rough black sand from
'Alelea crater, a few yards away. This crater erupted strongly again last
night, and by morning a big hill had formed there, about two or three
hundred feet high. Today with a long stick I wrote an SOS beside it about
where the meteorological hut had stood. An aircraft passed well to the
north at noon. Going westerly, might be from Samoa to Fiji. 'Alelea crater
has stopped erupting but makes an occasional roar like that of a lion, so
that people near it run for their lives. All wireless gear destroyed by lava
together with two big clocks and one alarm clock. Wireless masts covered
by thick layer of lava, which is about as thick as old Quensell's fence.
Wireless room also shared same fate. Living quarters worse as they were
too close to crater; lava covered up to half of cement tank. No one ever
dreamed that we were living and working between two huge craters. If
all the craters erupted at the same time, I, Ha'angana, Mr. Wolfgramm and
teacher (the last to leave Angaha) will be trapped inside wireless room
and no hope of escape. Luckily, and for some unknown reason, Angaha
craters seem to wait until we were all cleared from the danger area, then
they let everything go. If the eruption occurred between midnight and 6
a.m. there will be many loss of life. Although the material damage caused
by the eruption is too great, we thank the Almighty God from the bottom
of our hearts that through his kindness and unending love, no lives were
lost.

A harrowing ten days followed as the people of Niuafo'ou tried to
bring a semblance of order out of chaos. Six days after the disaster,
an American Catalina circled over the still steaming island and half
an hour later a radio signal to Nuku'alofa gave the first news of what
had happened. Plans for immediate relief operations were soon under
way and a decision later reached that everyone should be evacuated.
On the 21st December, the Union Steam Ship Company's islands
vessel *Matua* arrived to take them all to Nuku'alofa. Nature had at
last won its battle with the resilience of man.

Most of the 1,300 people settled on the island of 'Eua, rich, fertile
and hospitable, lying off the southern coast of Tongatapu. There in
exile they maintained the framework and ties of their old tribal

identities: 'The Niua people' - at once both strangers and brothers - to the men of 'Eua.

The problems of re-settlement continued. Twenty years after the evacuation of Niuafo'ou, an Evacuation Committee still met to arrange the occasional cutting and shipment of copra from the island and to administer the funds derived from its sale. The resumption of permanent habitation of Niuafo'ou remained officially forbidden until 1958.

During the preceding ten years, pressure had grown from the Niuafo'ou people for permission to return to their ancestral home - to their ruined houses and gardens, the trees and birds and fish, the graveyards of their forebears, and, above all, to resume the struggle for survival against the forces of nature. To permit them to return was an agonizing decision for Queen Salote and her Ministers to take.

In September 1958, the first party of 200 went back to their devastated island - an occasion of such sentimental significance that it is not easy for non-Polynesians fully to comprehend. Their island has a history of nine major eruptions in the past century. On each occasion, villages, paths, houses and gardens had been destroyed. Yet, they are there today, fearful but happy, no longer landless exiles, but back with their ancestors. The spirits of the dead have ceased to wander forlorn on the night winds of Niuafo'ou.

The story has a short postscript. The islanders of Niuafo'ou entertain a belief that the natural disasters which have befallen their homeland have been sent as punishment for wrong done or evil wrought by the chiefs of the island. Whether or not this is a Polynesian example of blame transference, the chiefly administrators of Tin Can Island are likely to continue to be as benevolent as human frailties permit.

*   *   *

You could argue, with good reason, that the tribulations of Tristan were nothing compared with those of Niuafo'ou. It would not be the point. What matters is the yearning, the irresistible determination of

forcibly transplanted island people to return home, no matter how
long they have to wait and no matter what the potential dangers may
be. That was the essential story of Niuafo'ou. It is still the key to and
the heart of Tristan da Cunha.

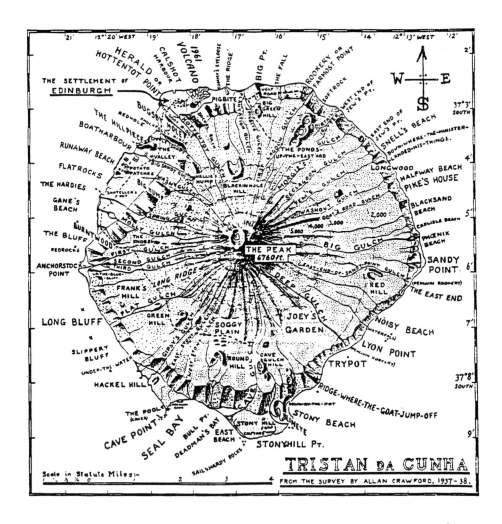

*Reproduced by kind permission of Allan Crawford from the survey he
made in 1937-8. The place names were collected from Islanders who
helped with the survey; they are either natural descriptions such Seal
Bay or they recalled events, i.e. 'Ridge-where-the-goat-jump-off.'*

CHAPTER 25

Voyage 6 North: Re-examination

The *RMS* turned round at Cape Town. The voyage south became the voyage north. From the container terminal, thirty-one eighteen ton containers were loaded with speed, silent efficiency and precision. In a twenty knot south-easterly, they came from a relay of delivery trucks via mountainous cranes. There was not a man in sight, except a handful in the hold of the *RMS*. Table Mountain was clear, resplendent. The Twelve Apostles nearby, proud in an unblemished blue sky.

The day before I had taken an all-day coach tour to Cape Point and the Cape of Good Hope Nature Reserve. Sections of the journey, notably Chapman's Peak Drive, match the best of the French Riviera. The panoramic sea cliffs are claimed to be the highest in the world; the roadside baboons perhaps the most frolicsome.

A bevy of young Saints boarded the *RMS* at Cape Town. There are thought to be about 8,000 St. Helenians resident in South Africa. The influx did much to reduce the average age of the passenger list. They buzzed with good spirits and vitality. Emblazoned in large letters across the bosom of one slim, dark-skinned beauty was

SEX INSTRUCTOR
No. 1 Lesson Free

I said: "Can I fix an appointment for lesson No. 1?"

She was clearly used to answering the question. "Sure," she replied. "Twelve noon today. Join the queue."

"What's that for - group therapy?"

"That's right, boy. You got it. Private lessons cost more, specially in Half Tree Hollow."

She erupted in laughter. A passing steward with drinks tray for the sun deck, said "Can I come and watch? Union rules don't let me join in."

The *RMS* may be all things to all men - and women. More so St. Helena itself. "The Saints are eminently promiscuous," said one well-heeled resident non-Saint whose sleek and non-dissenting wife is an equally well-heeled Saint. "Prostitution doesn't exist. There is no need for it. You can get it without paying. The Saints are free and easy about such things. You might even say it is a licentious society."

"Not so," said another. A woman this time. "Prostitution is there all right - with quiet subtlety."

My nerve failed as always at moments of investigative objectivity such as New Year's Eve when I went into the Consulate Hotel at about ten o'clock. For less than two minutes. Then I retreated and fled. There up the steps at the entrance and in the corridor inside were twenty or so young, bedecked, hopeful female Saints, single and alone with not a man in sight. Well, not a young one anyway. They looked *en masse* at me, and sighed together in orchestrated disappointment and disinterest.

I felt for them and their youthful yearnings for everything I was not. Hopefully, their time would come, later that New Year's Eve - or the next. Or the one after. Life has a lot further to go than you think, when you are sixteen. And a lot less, as you know, when you are somewhat more advanced along the road.

Radio Officer Bob Wilson was a seafaring loner. His models of old ships are exemplary and he is writing his autobiography. In the new *RMS* he presided over an array of computerized technology but lamented the passing of the compulsory skills of morse on merchant ships.

"I haven't been properly ashore at St. Helena or Ascension for years. I have far too much to do repairing everything that's broken down ... Some ships are lucky and some unlucky even when they are identical. The last two Union Castle ships - the 16,000 ton *Good Hope Castle* and the *Southampton Castle* were built in 1965 and withdrawn in 1978. The *Southampton Castle* was lucky. Nothing ever happened to it. The *Good Hope Castle* was unlucky. It had a terrible reputation. Not many wanted to work on her. I did because I got early promotion. She caught fire twice and the captain dropped dead in my presence just before our arrival in St. Helena. A large bull died on board about the same time. I don't think there was any connection. About 1975, there was a fire between St. Helena and Ascension. The ship was abandoned and later towed to Spain for a one year refit. I joined in Bilbao. We worked on the ship by day and stayed in an hotel at night. About ten of us contracted Legionnaire's Disease. You could say that wasn't the ship's fault but sailors are superstitious.

"The old *RMS* was a lucky ship. It ought to have sunk a couple of times - once when the forward hatch was flooded during a storm in the Falklands - but it never did. In the Falklands war, the Navy used to say to us 'you go first in the V formation and we'll follow' and we would do so. Nothing ever happened, even in the minefields."

"And what about the new *RMS*?" I asked.

"I don't know yet. It's too early to say, I suppose. But it is not so good when one engine goes on its maiden voyage. Yet Voyage 4 saw the *Oman Sea One* rescue and Voyage 6 has been a lucky voyage: comfortable seas after day one, excellent working conditions for cargo at St. Helena and Cape Town, unusually placid seas at Ascension and in the Bay of Biscay; and remarkably good fortune in the timing of our visit to Tristan with the port unworkable for three days prior to our arrival and then things settling down beautifully as we came in. They stayed like that throughout our stay but the bad weather returned the day after we sailed and the harbour was unworkable again ... I think that all aspiring clergymen should be required to spend about five years at sea before taking up holy orders. Then when they spoke about 'the wrath of God' they would know what they were talking about."

The old *RMS* under command of Captain Martin Smith suffered one such nightmare voyage in December 1978. Here is an extract from his report to Curnow Shipping:

The *RMS St. Helena* sailed on the midday tide on 6 December from Avonmouth bound for Ascension and St. Helena with 61 passengers and 436 tons of cargo. The weather forecasts were giving SE severe gales 9 for all southern sea areas. The *RMS* was bound south through Biscay and Finisterre, Trafalgar to Las Palmas in the Canary Isles for bunkers. We proceeded at slow speed towards Land's End in the lee of the Cornish peninsula monitoring the weather forecasts. The morning of 7 December saw no change in the weather pattern so it was decided to anchor in St. Ives Bay to await better conditions.

With 14 other ships the *RMS* swung to her anchor for 26 hours until an improvement was forecast. At 1030 hours on 8 December, the *RMS* weighed anchor and by noon was heading south off Wolf Rock into a force 5 with a rough sea and moderate swell taking spray over all the foredeck. By noon on Sunday 10 December when the *RMS* was 73' northwest of Finisterre having enjoyed a 'bouncing' ride across the Bay of Biscay, such that the Divine Service held at 1030 was held with everyone sitting during the hymns, the barometer started to fall quickly.

Without a check it fell 21mb in 8 hours which meant that by 1845 hours on Sunday evening the *RMS* was hove to into a very high sea and wind S 9/10. A very uncomfortable night followed. Meals were not served in the saloon but to cabins in a simplified form. By first light Monday, mountainous seas had built up and the mean wind speed had increased to force 10, which is 54 knots or 62 m.p.h. It was the mountainous sea all seafarers dread. The waves, 64 feet from trough to crest topped the foremast and swamped the ship as they ran relentlessly on. Although the ship was trying to make 7 knots ahead, the conditions were pushing her astern at 7 knots. During gusts the wind tore off the top of the seas and hurled them piecemeal like white dust obscuring vision completely. This marine version of Dante's Inferno lasted until 1500 hours on Monday afternoon when the wind veered and moderated to W 7. A general course for the Canaries could then be laid. During the height of the storm with large amounts of water sweeping the decks, the forepeak hatch was distorted and the forepeak store and cable lockers filled with water, much of the deck cargo was moved but very little lost. The Sappers' water filter cylinders broke out of their stow and started squaredancing with 6 cars in number 2 tweendeck which will necessitate a few 'cosmetic' repairs.

The passengers took the inconvenience and at times violent motion of the ship with great fortitude and some even enjoyed the wild spectacle, however, everyone was glad to step ashore in Las Palmas to shake the saltwater out of their ears when we arrived there at 1400 hours on

Thursday 14 December just 3½ days late. We learnt that the 37,000 ton German ship the *München* foundered in the same storm, together with six other vessels. She was some 300 miles to the west of the *RMS*. All shipping in the home trade Europe area was completely stopped for 4 days.

The *RMS* and her 3,150 tons rode the storm remarkably well proving herself well able to cope with such unusually severe and prolonged bad weather conditions. She was hove to in the storm for 20 hours during the worst of the weather. Her stay in Las Palmas was extended from the usual 8 hours to 26 hours so that various repairs could be done and at 1600 hours on Friday, 15 December the *RMS* left Las Palmas for Ascension with a determination to be at St. Helena before Christmas Day.

... 'And in Finisterre, gale force 8 increasing storm force 9 south veering south-west in the next twelve hours ...'

So it was that the new *RMS*, its officers, crew and passengers on Voyage 6 North endured one night in which the world of the ship turned upside down. The wind began to howl. The swell increased - long, slow and high. The ship pitched deep, slewed off course and back again. The spray crashed over the deck and, on the deeper plunges, smashed into the face of the bridge. Thence along the bridge deck and the liferafts and down over the sun deck. The ship shuddered and shivered as if a well-mannered beast had been awakened, cranky and ill-tempered. Whether that described an outwardly courteous Captain Bob Wyatt when at 6 a.m. one engine closed down, the steering went and the fire alarm bells momentarily surged through the ship, I do not know. Response was immediate and within minutes the ship was back on course, engine re-started and the false alarm cancelled.

"Great watch," said Chief Officer Bob Hone, looking exhausted. "The bridge hand chose that time to go below to get a cup of tea. I had to find four arms and twenty fingers to switch everything off. Roll on Cardiff!"

I had not slept for much of the night. It was nice to do so now as a kind of calm descended with the early morning light. It lasted across the Bay of Biscay in sunshine and gentle swells. The roaring tempest of the night had gone. Remember, they had said, the sea is master. But even maritime beasts have to sleep after they rant and rage.

There was one final unexpected burst of oceanic energy. An early morning force 8 developed off a murky and barely visible Land's End as the *RMS* began the final approaches to the Cardiff locks and the end of Voyage 6 North.

"Really?" said an unbelieving Cornish radio-watch coastguard. "It's all quiet on the western front here."

By the afternoon the gales were spent and as the evening began, the coastal lights of the Bristol Channel peeped shyly through the mist. At six, the Cardiff pilot clambered up the forward port ladder, walked up to the bridge and said "Welcome to Wales" in English and Welsh.

For Captain Bob Wyatt it was a melancholy occasion. Closely following his colleague Martin Smith, he had been with Curnow Shipping as joint Master of the old *RMS* and now the new, since soon after the company's operations to St. Helena began in 1977. His attachment to the sea and to the islands and people of St. Helena and Tristan da Cunha had become his life. Now, at 50, it was all to end in premature retirement. He had failed to meet the stringent British medical maritime standard for eyesight. He could no longer be in command at sea.

There had been a succession of emotional farewells - at Ascension, by the crew at the Consulate Hotel in St. Helena, by the officers and passengers separately on board and at Plantation House by the Governor and Delia Hoole with an assembly of specially chosen guests from the Government and people of St. Helena and the *RMS*.

"We are saying goodbye to a true friend of St. Helena," a Saint said to me. "Not just to Captain Wyatt of the *RMS*."

"I didn't think that retiring would be such hard work," said a stretched Robert Henry Wyatt of Somerset, in response to a farewell eulogy by Alan Hoole. "What I shall miss most is the comradeship of my colleagues on the ship."

His public duties were, however, not quite over. There was his last Sunday service. And he presided for the last time as King

Neptune in the crossing the line ceremony as the ship passed the Equator on its journey home. There was the usual horseplay and merriment; but Bob Hone and his officer colleagues had devised a twist at the end. On this occasion, they gathered up and threw the retiring King Neptune into the swimming pool. He had not been forewarned. As he surfaced, crown gone, sceptre askew, robe lying flat on ice cream topped water and surrounded by sausage-type intestines, Bob Wyatt cried out in anguish

"Good God. I've lost me script!"

In the darkness of a chill winter's night the *RMS* was secure at her Cardiff berth at 7.40 p.m. on Tuesday, 19th February, 1992. Then it was that Bob Wyatt gave his last command at sea:

FINISHED WITH ENGINES

And turned away. He had no further need of that script. Voyage 6 South and North of the *RMS St. Helena* was over.

CHAPTER 26

Birth of a Ship

The bottom line - so goes the cliché - is this: no other isolated dependent territory island community - British or otherwise - has been served and serviced by its own given and 'bespoke-tailored' passenger cargo ship. One for which, neither directly nor indirectly, has it had to pay. But one in which there is pride of ownership and thus responsibility for operating style and preferment.

The story begins at the end of another: the demise of the great Union Castle liners which ran from Britain to South Africa. There was a time when these ships sailed out of Southampton at 4 p.m. each Thursday via the Canaries to Cape Town, thence round the south-east coast to Port Elizabeth, East London and Durban before turning round and retracing their journey. In the larger ships, the passengers were carefully segregated in first and tourist classes. Those in one had no access to or contact with those in another. The rich and the privileged were cocooned in the luxury of shipboard cultural indulgence, their God-given status recognised and reinforced extra-territorially.

Like New Zealand, the Republic of South Africa is at the end of the antipodean line, albeit of a great land and not ocean mass. As white South Africans increasingly had nowhere to go that they found welcoming and compatible in their own continent, they looked to the sea round their coasts. Many of the affluent and leisured took passage from the Cape to Durban in order to escape the claustrophobia of the land; and in doing so, found that they could, unexpectedly, often do the journey more quickly than by rail.

The last of the passenger mailships on the north-south run were the Safmarine *SA Vaal* which made her final voyage in September 1977 and the *Southampton Castle* whose last voyage ended at Southampton on 24th October, 1977. The great raj-like oceanic odysseys to the Cape had come to an end, 120 years after the Union Castle service had started. But while they lasted, on many voyages, the ships put in to Jamestown. The passengers liked it and so did the Saints. The ships brought mail, cargo, passage in and out and brief business on ship days for those who conveyed visitors to the Napoleonic shrine at Longwood. The little post office was stretched to cope as counter sales and philatelic interest in St. Helena increased.

The demise of the great passenger liners did not affect only the United Kingdom-South Africa run. Gradually over a decade or so, P and O, Shaw Savill, Matson, Royal Rotterdam Lloyd, even the latecomers like Lloyd Triestino and Flotto Lauro, came to schedule their last Australasian, Round the Cape, Panama and Suez sailings. So went to the scrapyards and into maritime history, ships with names like *Oriana, Arcadia, Iberia, Strathnaver, Chusan, Strathaird, Orsova, Andes, Oronsay, Dominion Monarch, Marconi, Oranje, Monterey, Mariposa* and the trans-Atlantic liners of White Star, Cunard and Canadian Pacific. Conquest by the jet engine, mass air travel, high fuel prices and crippling inflation was complete. Worldwide trunk route passenger sea travel was dead, killed off by impossible operating and replacement costs. Not altogether surprising when, for example, the Matson Pacific ships carried a 2-1 crew-passenger ratio for five hundred first class passengers.

There was another equally painful parallel consequence: the slow but inevitable extinction of the British merchant navy. Flags of convenience proliferated - Liberia, Cyprus, Panama, Vanuatu, The Bahamas, Greece and so on. The age of elegance and leisure at sea and a tradition of constructing fine ships in British shipyards had vanished. Overnight it seemed to some, as unemployment bit deep and bitter.

Then what appeared to be the final indignity and insult to the British ship-building and repair industry: Cunard took its *QE II* to Bremen and its cruise ships to Malta for refit because British bids were too high and too slow; and in the Bahamas, Nassau replaced Southampton as the port of registry for its latter-day mass market cruise ships.

The British Government was in one case compelled to consider what it should do, reacting as governments do so reluctantly to problems which everyone else has anticipated. A small Cornish shipping company believed that it knew how best to relate to the needs of a comparably small isolated South Atlantic island people. It was headed by Andrew Bell, a man of street-wise sensitivity and tenacity; plus years at sea with the Blue Funnel Line before he began to wrestle with their problems in West Africa from the insecure - and losing - base in the Port Harcourt of Biafra during the Nigerian Civil War.

"It served me right I suppose," he says reflectively "because I had confidently predicted to my employers that the persuasively logical reasons why there would be no such war meant quite clearly that it would not happen. It was my first and hardest lesson of the unwisdom of rationalising another people's culture and problems through the ways of thinking of one's own."

In the face of fierce competition, Andrew Bell and Curnow won the shipping management contract to St. Helena in 1977. The St. Helena Shipping Company was born; and Porthleven in South Cornwall was its birthplace. How it came to be there is a family story of Yorkshire woollen mills, thence Cornwall and Australia and, for Bell, born beside Manly Beach in Sydney, back to Porthleven via Blue Funnel.

Tenacity and determination are great human qualities - except in the perception of those who possess neither and rate conformity and security as more comfortingly reassuring on the journey home from Whitehall to Watford.

Ten years later - strange as you may think it - there was a singular exception in the Whitehall corridors of modest power. It was that desk officer for St. Helena at the Overseas Development Administration at Eland House in London from 1984 to 1989: Clive Warren. Temperamentally and psychologically, he and Andrew Bell had more in common than either perhaps first realised when official accountability and commercial enterprise began - through these two apparently quite different men - to come together on the quest for a new ship for St. Helena. Ignore the chemistry between the two, whatever the disagreements, and you ignore the reality. The reality is that without both the new ship might not have been. They were not operating together - far from it at times when official distancing from commercial probing was essential. Yet their objectives were essentially the same - to establish a shipping service for the people of St. Helena which would be reliable and safe: one in which the Saints could take pride.

The first ship - now generally known on St. Helena as 'the old *RMS*' - was the 3,150 ton vessel *Northland Prince*, built in Vancouver in 1963 for the British Columbia-Alaska coastal trade. She had a service speed of fourteen knots but only a single screw; and she was not, of course designed for the rigours of the South Atlantic or indeed the Antarctic. But the general specifications seemed close to ideal for the time.

The ship was bought for £1 million in the autumn of 1977; given a £1 million refit; and formally re-named *St. Helena* by Princess Margaret. She set off on her maiden voyage in the service of the island of St. Helena and its people on 13th September, 1978. It was the first of 69 round voyages to the South Atlantic.

One maiden voyage passenger was Alan Hoole, en route to take up appointment as the island's Attorney General. He has one wry memory of his time there. "On 1st April, 1982," he told me, "the Governor, John Massingham, had to leave for medical treatment. The Chief Secretary was on leave; the Colonial Treasurer had only just arrived; and I was the next in line to act as Governor."

"You'll be all right," said the departing Massingham. "I am sure that everything will be nice and quiet while I am away."

It was an April Fool's Day prognosis. Twenty-four hours later, Argentina invaded the Falklands Islands. War had come to the South Atlantic - and St. Helena was the closest British territory.

The old *RMS* was immediately requisitioned. In a week, she was converted at Portsmouth to a minesweeper support ship. Thus

Curnow Shipping, their officers and general sea staff, British and Saints alike, went to war; and faced the awesome adjustments demanded of them. The ship took part with distinction in the Falklands campaign until her release in July 1983. She returned in September that year - with more conviction than capability - to the St. Helena mail-passenger-cargo run. She carried only seventy-six passengers in cabins and was consistently fully booked. Saints, shuttling to Ascension and back, mostly travelled in unacceptable discomfort on deck. Breakdowns and delays were beginning to occur.

Undeniably, her future as the island's only regular link with the outside world was limited. A newer, larger and technically superior vessel would be needed sooner rather than later; and official files in The Castle, the Foreign and Commonwealth Office and the Overseas Development Administration grew thick with erudite dissections of the alternatives facing the Governments of Britain and St. Helena. As the power play proceeded, Andrew Bell stood at this stage in the wings, putting in his contribution from time to time and then retreating to Porthleven to ponder the ways of Whitehall, its officials and their political masters.

For one important argument had to be tackled head on: why should the British Government meet the bill for a new ship at all? This was after all the hey-day of seemingly impregnable Thatcherism, the 'marketplace' approach prevailed and the Treasury's 'Value for Money' concept for public expenditure which Margaret Thatcher had joyfully embraced, hardly extended to financing the construction of a government-owned ship to run a loss-leader subsidised service to a tiny forgotten relic of empire. But 'forgotten' was at least part of the argument that began to turn the tide of political thinking and, if there is such a thing, political conscience. For in the mid-eighties St. Helena - or rather the British Government's supposed attitude of indifference to or disinterest in it - was getting a bad press. There had been an Anglia TV film severely critical of neglect of St. Helena and its people, Sir Bernard Braine in the vanguard; and Simon Winchester had pronounced judgement in his *Outposts* of 1985 about this 'forlorn little island':

> This pinpoint of inaccessibility, unbelievably remote was once a place of significance; it is now, to Britain, of no consequence whatsoever, is steadfastly ignored and neglected by a mother country to whom her natives look in vain for succour and friendship. It has been turned, in consequence, into what one recent visitor called 'an Imperial slum.'
>
> One cannot come away from St. Helena without shaking one's head and muttering that something must be done; but nothing has been, nothing is, nothing ever will be done - under the suzerainty of Britain, at least. The story of St. Helena is a tragedy of decay and isolation, poverty and ruin, and all played by a principal cast of proud and enchanting islanders, and in their home of magical beauty. (But a recent decision taken in London, taking the daily running of the island away from the Foreign Office, may yet improve matters).

Did all this doom-and-gloom pessimism - and that of others - have any effect? I am inclined to think that it may well have done. Timothy Raison was Minister for Overseas Development at the time; and he was seemingly uncomfortable and defensive in the Anglia TV film on St. Helena. He would not be today; and the beginnings of change for the better were established during his time in office. Forward financial commitments were being made: not least this special one, made known by Governor Dick Baker in a broadcast on Radio St. Helena on 21st May, 1986 (St. Helena Day):

> In a speech about the United Kingdom shipbuilding industry in the House of Commons today, the Secretary of State for Trade and Industry, Mr. Paul Channon, with the agreement of the Minister of Overseas Development, Mr. Timothy Raison, announced that the Government intends to finance from the aid programme a newly-built ship to provide adequate service for St. Helena. The ship will be built in a United Kingdom shipyard ... This announcement represents a firm commitment by Her Majesty's Government to build a new ship for St. Helena. The precise type, specifications and size of the ship will be decided shortly and we in St. Helena will be consulted ...

It was one thing for that announcement to be made in the House of Commons in London. It had been quite another - in those pre-direct dial telephone days - to get it through to the island itself on St. Helena Day.

Clive Warren was at home in Hertfordshire when he received confirmation in the early evening that the ministerial statement had been duly delivered at Westminster. What happened next was what finally convinced him that something had to be done about St. Helena's telecommunications system.

He called British Telecom and asked the operator for a person-to-person call to the Governor of St. Helena. At first there was silence. Then

"You are wanting the Governor of somewhere?"

"Yes I am. This is an official call and I want the Governor. His name is Dick Baker."

"I see. The Governor's name is Dick Baker and you are wanting to speak with him."

"Yes."

"Right. I'll see what I can do ... Governor of where?"

"St. Helena. I want a call to St. Helena. To the Governor."

"St. Helena, sir? Where is that?"

"It is an island in the South Atlantic Ocean."

"I haven't heard of that one, sir. I'll have to look it up."

"You do it through Ascension Island."

"Ascension Island? Where is that?"

"That's in the South Atlantic too."

"Right, sir. I am calling you back."

Ten minutes later he duly did so with a momentous announcement: "I'm sorry, sir. I have spoken with Ascension Island and they tell me that St. Helena is closed now."

Clive Warren exploded. "Well they'll jolly soon open up again when they know what I've got to tell them. So please find a way of getting them to do so pronto."

Another ten minutes went by. Then the operator came back again.

"Somebody in Ascension," he said, "is contacting somebody on St. Helena by ham radio to arrange for the telephone service on St. Helena to open up again for you. So here's hoping."

Warren looked at his watch. It was 7.30 p.m. in the UK; 6.30 p.m. on St. Helena. Everyone at The Briars had gone to a St. Helena Day party maybe. An hour or so later, a grateful Dick Baker came on the fade and static-prone line to write down Clive Warren's news, minutes before he was due to go on the air with his St. Helena Day message on the island's radio station. It had been touch and go; but for the Saints it was some message.

Then on 13th December, 1986, Dick Baker went again to Radio St. Helena, this time to give outline details of the new ship which had been agreed between ODA and the Government of St. Helena.

"It will be a mixed passenger-supply vessel with more cargo and passengers, none being carried on deck. It is estimated that £44m will be spent over twenty-three years, that is the cost of building the vessel and the annual subsidy required to run it for twenty years. This may or may not change slightly as time goes by ..."

The optimistic financial caution at the time was understandable; and change the estimates did, not slightly but so drastically and unconventionally that the ship's design construction and potential cost became a living nightmare for Clive Warren and his colleagues. That it was completed at all is one of the triumphs of an oft-maligned ODA. It very nearly never happened. The reasons are essentially simple and had been foreshadowed in early internal warnings to the British Government ministers of the day.

In July 1990, the Comptroller and Auditor General of the National Audit Office reported to the British Parliament the results of an examination into the procurement and costs of the new ship for St. Helena. The report did not make for pleasant reading. Even so, it made no direct comment on the policy decision by ministers to put the construction to Scotland - the key factor in the dismal equation - other than to say that it made none. The reason is that ministerial policy decisions are not subject to scrutiny, evaluation or general comment in an Audit Office report to the Public Accounts Committee of the House of Commons. The implications were, however, clear.

The press release summary of the thirty-four paragraph report was as follows:

In 1986 the UK Government announced its intention of replacing the existing vessel, which was reaching the end of its operational life. During 1987 the Overseas Development Administration (ODA) obtained tenders to build a new vessel. The lowest tender was submitted by Hall Russell of Aberdeen but the company was unable to provide an adequate financial guarantee. ODA's consultants advised that, without a further order (which it later obtained) or an increase in the tender price, Hall Russell would require an injection of capital to complete the St. Helena ship; and that in such circumstances, special financial terms should be agreed. ODA therefore preferred another tender.

The Industry Department for Scotland were not convinced that there were adequate grounds for setting aside Hall Russell's bid. Whilst they noted the ODA's view that it was impossible to be certain of the additional costs if Hall Russell failed, the Department considered on the basis of the consultants advice that these would not exceed £0.2 million. The ODA agreed to accept Hall Russell's bid after the Scottish office offered to meet any extra costs of completing the St. Helena above their preferred tender. Although Hall Russell secured a further order, its financial situation deteriorated and a year later it was put into receivership.* At that time the *St. Helena* was one-third complete.

The ODA invited tenders for the completion of the ship and their choice narrowed to Zenta Engineering Ltd. and A &P Appledore Ltd. Both proposed completion in the Hall Russell yard, which they would purchase from the Receivers. On several key issues the ODA judged Appledore as a significantly better risk, although its tender was £1.5 million higher. The Industry Department for Scotland, however, favoured Zenta on cost and other grounds. During negotiations the gap between the tenders narrowed to £0.9 million.

Zenta made an offer to purchase the shipyard, not conditional on obtaining the *St.Helena* contract. Appledore agreed to improve on Zenta's bid by a small amount, provided that ODA accepted an increase of £0.6 million in its tender price. The ODA agreed, considering this to be the best way of protecting the Government's position.

The ship was launched in October 1989 and is scheduled to enter service

*Reportedly with debts of several million pounds owed to over eighty creditors

in August 1990, eight months late. The total cost of the ship is now estimated at £32.3 million, net of guarantees called in, an increase of £12.8 million (66 per cent) over the original contract price.

The NAO found that the Administration used their normal procedures for this aid project and took appropriate specialist advice. As a result of the decision to accept the Hall Russell tender, an additional £11 million has been committed from Government funds and continued employment was provided to the workforce of 500, of whom 475 remain employed at the yard, with associated employment effects on the local economy. More generally the National Audit Office highlighted a number of principles for project assessment and management arising from this case.

The serpentine convolutions concealed within this deadpan summary did not escape newspaper editors. '£13m BLUNDER IN SHIP ORDER' proclaimed *The Guardian* and blamed the then Scottish Secretary, Malcolm Rifkind, for ordering the ship from a Scottish yard, which ministers knew could go bankrupt, instead of Lowestoft or Clydeside. "MP URGES HALL RUSSELL PROBE' said the *Aberdeen Evening Express*. 'IT'S THE GREAT SHIP CONTRACT BLUNDER' trumpeted the *Bristol Evening Post*. 'SAVING 500 ABERDEEN JOBS COST THE TAXPAYER £12.8m' said the caption to an article by *The Scotsman* business editor.

The heart of the matter was none of this. It was how and in what circumstances did the negotiations with the Receiver result in an outcome which safeguarded St. Helena's embryonic new lifeline (in which ODA had already invested some £7,200,000) while minimising the additional cost of completion to the quality standard needed. The negotiations were long and arduous, with more than the usual supply of midnight oil (and sandwiches) being consumed in the ODA 'corridors of power.' Over many tortuous months, Clive Warren's tiny St. Helena section, with sustained and sustaining support from Robin Marriott, at the Crown Agentstook the brunt of it. Between them, they helped salvage St. Helena's steel hulk in an Aberdeen shipyard from the legal, technical and financial quagmire into which it was in daily danger of sinking without ever sailing to the vast expanses of the Atlantic Ocean. Indeed, at that time the whole proposition might have seemed to faint-hearted officialdom as if the likelihood of a new second ship for St. Helena was not all that far from Dr. Johnson's view of the prospects for second marriage: 'A triumph of hope over experience.'

The full details of what exactly went on over those months in 1988 and 1989 may never be fully revealed. Suffice to say that Frank Blin, the Receiver on the other end of the negotiations, later cited the Hall Russell receivership as his own biggest test thus far. Interviewed by *The Scotsman* newspaper, Blin reportedly said, 'That taught me a real lesson about dealing with the politics of life. Nobody will know, other than my law agent who walked with me every day, the tight-rope we were treading at the time.' My hunch is that Clive Warren and Robin Marriott know as well - but they're not telling either!

But of this, I am personally certain: without Clive Warren and his colleagues it is doubtful whether the *RMS St. Helena* would have been built to the standards that it has; and it might not have been completed at all. In an atmosphere of cost-cutting consciousness and with the massive additional costs involved in completing the *RMS* - albeit as the media contended largely because of ministerial misjudgment in the first place - the political will to proceed with the commitment to the specifications agreed with the Government of St. Helena could have faltered or even been put into permanent reverse. There would have been reason - including perhaps an easier ride in the House of Commons - to review the whole question 'in the light of considerations not known to ministers when the first financial commitments were made,' etc. etc.

Thanks principally to the tenacity of a handful of dedicated officials, that did not happen. And St. Helena has its fine new ship.

This is how it is described by Curnow Shipping:

The *RMS St. Helena* is a working ship. Her prime purpose is to carry cargo and mail efficiently, and passengers comfortably and reliably: a purpose which the St. Helena Shipping Company and Curnow Shipping, who manage the line, have accomplished for more than fifteen years.

The ship, designed to carry 20 foot containers, also has two tanks for cargo oil, and a purpose built area for carrying livestock and pets in reasonable comfort, sheltered from the elements.

The *RMS St. Helena* with her stabilisers, modern facilities and air conditioning, provides 128 passenger berths in two, three and four berth cabins: each with its own shower, wash basin and toilet. A comfortable lounge and bar, sun lounge and swimming pool, dining saloon and shop, small library and self-service laundry, ship's hospital ward and doctor, ensure that passengers have all the comforts of a first class hotel.

Designed by Three Quays Marine Services, London (member of the P & O Group).

Built by A & P Appledore (Aberdeen) Limited.

Launched 31st October, 1989 by HRH The Prince Andrew, Duke of York.

Delivered 26th October, 1990.

Temporarily registered in London.

U.K. and St. Helenian officers and crew.

Captain Martin Smith was in command of the new ship for Voyage 1 South and her first landfall at St. Helena. Here are brief extracts from his report:

After the 4th set of sea trails the v/1 was accepted and handed over to managers, Curnow Shipping, at 1415 hours Friday, 26th October, 1990. The 2nd Mate, Rodney Young, symbolically accepted the ship on behalf of St. Helena island. The ship was completed 2 years 10 months after the initial order and 5 days short of a year after her launch by HRH The Prince Andrew, Duke of York. More significantly she was 3 months late on her contractual delivery date of 31st July. After a brief 'Thank you and Farewell' lunchtime party, the ship made ready to leave Aberdeen on the 7 p.m. tide, with a complement of 26 and 12 supernumeraries.

The ship sailed for Falmouth and Cardiff which was to be her United Kingdom home port. She berthed on Sunday 11th November 1990. Next day, for the first and only time, the old *RMS* and the new *RMS* met and tied up beside each other. As Martin Smith described it:

With Captain Wyatt in command, the '*Old RMS*' came through the locks

to a siren welcome at 1415 hours Monday 12th November and berthed
port side to astern of the *'New RMS.'*

The crew transferred that evening and all hands attended a very touching
service of dedication and blessing by the Rev. Michael Houghton in the
sun lounge. After the service the assembled ship's company were
appraised of the full content of the remaining 4 days in port before sailing
on the maiden voyage. A period of intense activity not only loading the
cargo and preparing the ship for passengers and the voyage, but also a full
work-up of the crew in all the familiarisation and safety drill procedures
to make the crew and ship fit and safe to go to sea. The sailing day was
put back 24 hours in order to facilitate a proper work-up and do the final
DTI survey items and emergency drills.

The ship sailed from Cardiff at 6 p.m. on Friday 16th November.
Voyage 1 South had begun. As the news spread throughout St.
Helena, excitement mounted. Preparations for a grand welcome were
put in hand. The Government declared that arrival day would be a
public holiday. Just as well. Not that it would have made much
difference. Everyone would have gone anyway.

Martin Smith again:

With instructions to arrive at St. Helena at 0900 hours promptly for a
public welcome on Friday 30th November, we decided to make for West
Point to hide under Man and Horse Cliffs at sunrise on 30th November to
dress ship and made a surprise arrival off West Rocks, James Bay at 0900
hours having hugged the coast for the 6 mile journey. The welcome was
colourful as it was noisy and a flotilla of boats escorted and circled the
ship as we anchored at 0922 hours. 96 passengers, 1 dog, mail and
baggage were landed in the forenoon and the ship made ready for 'open
ship' 1300 to 1800 hours. We estimate that approximately 2,300 islanders
came out to the ship in the 5 hour period, everyone who was on the wharf,
in fact.

A week later on 7th December 1990 at 5p per copy the *St. Helena News* was still breathless with excitement.

A DREAM BECOMES REALITY!

FRIDAY, 30TH November 1990 was a very special day for the people of St. Helena. Special because they witnessed the arrival of the maiden voyage of the new *RMS St. Helena*, built in Aberdeen, Scotland by A & P Appledore.

At 6 a.m., in rather dismal weather, the vessel was seen at the western side of the Island hoisting her flags in preparation for her grand entry into James Bay. It was a spectacular sight when she crossed the harbour in front of some two thousand or more people congregated along the quayside as well as the old Battery at the top of Ladder Hill to witness this historic occasion.

The reception she received was overwhelming! On her final approach to her anchorage, she was received by a flotilla of boats very colourfully displayed with flags gently blowing to and fro in the early morning breeze. A large quantity of balloons were also released from the boats brightening the sky.

The entire Wharf was colourfully decorated with bunting and coloured lights. The flagpole at Ladder Hill, overlooking Jamestown was also decorated with flags and coloured lights which for the first time made that particular area look so beautiful.

When the vessel anchored, the Prince Andrew School choir accompanied by the Gettogethers Orchestra sang a welcome song. The perfect harmony of both choir and orchestra were evidence of many hours of practice ...

An estimated two thousand people visited the ship and were given guided tours by the officers and crew. Everyone's impression was the same; a truly magnificent ship ...

The vessel is equipped with the most modern technology found on any ship today. The bridge is fully computerised and controls practically every part of the vessel; really Hi-tech stuff!

Our dream has finally become a reality. May she be successful in all her travels.

GOD BLESS OUR NEW RMS!!!

Well, God must have been slumbering or otherwise preoccupied when, at 0310 hours on Saturday 5th January, 1991, near Lisbon on Voyage 1 North 'the starboard engine destroyed itself with a con-rod breaking and smashing everything in reach. Third Engineer Wally Croston pressed the emergency stop button just two seconds after the automatic shut down had been activated.' A major disaster was narrowly averted.

Using the port engine, shaft and propeller only, the *RMS* limped into Lisbon where a bevy of Lloyds and Salvage surveyors with a Mirrlees engine representative were already assembled. The passengers were flown home and the ship set off with cautious circumspection to Falmouth for repairs and engine replacement. She arrived at 8 a.m. on Sunday, 20th January. 'The voyage' wrote Martin Smith 'lasted nine weeks and three days, just two weeks longer than planned. A disappointing end to an otherwise reasonably successful maiden voyage.'

Yet it was only one voyage. The timetable for the ship is planned two years ahead. It provides for six round trip voyages in twelve months with twenty four calls at St. Helena in each such period. As of December 1991, the passenger service was fully booked in 1992 and 1993; and there was one booking for 1996.

Andrew Bell and his colleagues at Curnow Shipping are especially proud of two things: for the first time in 1991 - the total annual ODA subsidy for the operation of the *RMS* was less than £1m (£920,000), against an increase in revenue of over £1 million. It is true that in achieving this, there were some staff redundancies and pay adjustments; but it was achieved in only six voyages of the new ship.

The company's proudest achievement has, however, been the training and promotion of Saints to increasing shipboard responsibility 'entirely,' he says 'without government requirement or pressure.' One outstanding example is now First Mate Rodney Young - School Bus - who could be on the threshold of obtaining a master's certificate. Myron Benjamin, Chief Engineer in waiting, is another. So too is Mark Williams, also a qualified Chief Engineer, who was seconded in 1992 to another set of islands, The Shetlands - as an acting Superintendent Engineer for their intra-archipelagic ferry services.

There seems little doubt that the day is in sight when the ship that was a gift by Britain to the government and people of St. Helena will be staffed by officers and crew all of whom are Saints.

Their first voyage will be one to remember.

CHAPTER 27

The Contract

In 1995 Curnow Shipping will be twenty years old. Its continuing connections with St. Helena go back to 1977. Andrew Bell has been at the Portleven helm throughout; but it has not, as we know, all been plain sailing.

He and everyone else on board Voyage 6 and on St. Helena were well aware that the contract for the future operation of the ship would soon be put out by ODA to public tender. Curnow, its land and sea-going staff, would be under extra non-maritime pressures. They might begin with some advantages: they had been closely associated with the design and construction of the new ship; and they had been managing and operating it since Voyage 1. Their safety record was second to none; the crew training programme spoke for itself; and the reliability of the scheduled service since the early misbehaviour of the engines on the maiden voyage (not a management responsibility) were beyond criticism.

All this was fine - so far as it went. Curnow might start the race on the inside track, but it could not conceivably afford to take the result for granted. All aspects of their performance would be subject to severe and critical scrutiny, as well as their proposals for the future. There was support for the company on St. Helena itself and from Saints in Britain - some indeed of the 'better the devil you know' kind. But there was critical opposition. It was articulated, perhaps orchestrated, by a Legislative Councillor who considered that it was time for change to operational management by a British international shipping company such as Cunard or P and O. It was a plausible approach - if either could be attracted by the contract terms on offer. In the event, a number of smaller British and non-British companies were initially interested; but no major shipping companies put in bids.

There was an element of *déjà vu* for Andrew Bell as he began the process of preparing his latest battle campaign to defeat potential competitors. An element only because, while he had indeed been through it all before, an even tougher commercial atmosphere now prevailed. Recognition and acceptance of this was the key to the realism needed to plan the St. Helena service of the future and to succeed in being chosen to run it, with or without subsidy.

In response to the ODA advertisement, twenty-four companies initially expressed interest in tendering. The tender documents reached them on 10th June 1992. The ship was opened for comprehensive inspection by all potential tenderers at Cardiff on 17th June. Some had travelled on the ship from Tenerife - to appraise the beating heart from within the body and perhaps to escape a miserable English summer. The 'viewing' was organised by David Roberts, promoted to join Martin Smith as master on the retirement of Bob Wyatt. Representatives from sixteen companies turned up. There was a four hour briefing session by the ODA shipping consultant in the afternoon. He faced a barrage of questions about the tender conditions and ODA policy in respect of the service.

Six days later, the closing date for tenders was extended from 10th July to 24th July. Six tenderers were to be short-listed and invited to appear before an official selection committee in London in early September. An important member of that committee was Alan Hoole. His constitutional responsibilities for shipping had been well to the forefront of his mind for many months. He arrived with Delia at Brize Norton by RAF flight from Ascension Island on Wednesday 8th July. Before his departure from St. Helena, he had released a detailed public statement about the tender process and the conditions of it. He predicted that the successful tenderer might not be known until about the end of September. That forecast was to prove to be entirely accurate.

On the morning of 24th July, Simon Sugrue (a founding director of Curnow Shipping) arrived at the entrance to the Crown Agents offices at Sutton in Surrey. He had some rather important documents to hand over: the Curnow tender bid for the St. Helena shipping contract. It was in ten volumes, each made up of 312 pages and each accompanied by what Andrew Bell described as an 'Executive Summary, what the company had achieved since 1977 and what was thus the "best buy." One paragraph heading said all that Curnow stood for:

'The Vital Trinity of Priorities:
Safety, People, Cost.'

For each of the shortlisted tenderers, there would be twenty minutes for the presentation itself; ninety minutes for tender committee questions; and ten minutes for questions by the tenderer.

Andrew Bell was cautiously optimistic after the Curnow appearance. "The atmosphere was splendid," he said. "We had an excellent reception. Good humour prevailed throughout. Even Ron White (Clive Warren's successor on the ODA St. Helena desk) laughed at our pleasantries!"

That was all very well, significant or not. Others had to be heard, the arguments sifted, the proposals analysed and debated, the case prepared for ministers. So what was the bottom line priority: safety, cost, sea-staff training and pay, schedule reliability, cargo delivery, maintenance standards, passenger comfort? Or all of them? How did the track records of the applicants compare? Was the subsidy to be phased out? If so, how and over what period of time? Whose interests should come first? Those of a British government department or the people of an isolated British colony? Should the ship have a flag of convenience registration with a cut-price Filipino crew on short-term contracts with no long-term dedication to the interests of St. Helena? What was the political approach to all this? What did the British Government stand for; and what were the officials of the FCO and ODA really after?

It seemed to me that Alan Hoole might have more than a barnyard fight on his hands. There were questions of principle to be addressed and resolved. For him, I had no doubt, the vital component was people: the people of St. Helena, whose ship it was and in whose name it sailed the waters of the Atlantic.

On Sunday 13th September, Alan and Delia Hoole flew from London to join the *RMS* at Cape Town. The contract decision was tucked securely away in the sealed papers he was carrying. ... Sealed lips too. Hoole well knew that he was in the hands of those whose fate, and that of their wives and children, lay within those papers. Martin Smith, his officers and crew were well aware of it also - and, nerves on edge, of the need for patience and silence. Sailors are rather good at both, when it is required of them. So for five days in the presence of the man who carried the decision with him, the unmentionable was unmentioned.

But there was a point when everyone on board the *RMS* thought that it was about to be. From time to time, Curnow has carried officers of the Royal Navy on voyages of familiarisation. This was one of them. Two nights out from St. Helena, a full scale RN mess dinner ritual was staged for the edification and entertainment of the passengers. The Bishop of St. Helena not only sang the grace but, it seems, danced it as well. Alan Hoole, Governor and Commander in Chief, was the guest of honour and principal speaker. He decided to play a little game with his audience.

As he stood to speak, he produced a bundle of official papers and assumed an air of portentous seriousness. "You will understand that this has not been an easy speech to prepare. It has taken a long time to write because it is important, of course, that I do justice to what has been happening over recent months ..."

There was rapt silence in the packed *RMS* dining saloon. Everyone present thought 'this is it. He is about to tell us who has won the contract. Oh boy.'

Alan Hoole looked slowly round at the anxious faces, turned back to his papers and said "I want to assure you that the competition has been fairly conducted and that the decision ..." He paused. "Just a minute. I do apologise. That's not the speech for the mess dinner.

That's another one. Let me see. Here we are." He shuffled his papers, looked around once more and began again.

My assumption was that the formal announcement would be made by the Governor at an early meeting with his Executive Council at The Castle, probably on Wednesday 23rd September; that an agreed public statement would follow; and that, at the same time, all tenderers would be advised of the outcome of their bids by ODA in London. "Praise be," Alan Hoole, unlike the less fortunate Dick Baker, might well have said, "for instant international direct dialling and the fax."

On the evening of Thursday 24th September, I took the train to London and went to the Queen Elizabeth Hall. Not this time for Mozart or Schubert or Haydn but for a jazz concert of splendid re-creations of the music of the so-called Dr. Jazz: Jelly Roll Morton and his Red Hot Peppers. By the interval, the performance was running late. I dialled home to clock in about the train arrangements. My wife answered "Andrew Bell called," said Margaret. "Curnow has won the St. Helena shipping contract."

"That's good. He will be delighted. I am, too. I will ring him in the morning."

I went back into the auditorium. The latter-day Red Hot Peppers launched into a spirited 'Steamboat Stomp.' It seemed kind of appropriate.

*   *   *

Tuesday 22nd December was cold and clear in Cardiff. There had been a frost overnight - as well as policemen with sniffer dogs in lounges, cabins, lockers and offices throughout the ship. Every nook and cranny is the cliché. In the morning, the frogmen came in their wet suits, plunged below the surface and went over the hull, plate by plate. The thick, sludge-like water was less than inviting. For a time, there seemed to be more security men on board than staff.

The Duke of York flew in by helicopter and was met by Her Majesty's Lord-Lieutenant for South Glamorgan. Andrew Bell became ADC for the day and undertook the introduction of the guests

assembled in the forward lounge for a pre-lunch reception. Bishop
James Johnson, former Bishop of St. Helena, caught his eye.

"May I introduce the first Saint to become a Bishop," he said.

Prince Andrew's eyes glittered.

"Good grief," he said "The mind boggles. Sounds like demotion
to me." He roared with laughter. So did we all, including the Saintly
Bishop.

CHAPTER 28

'Let Go Fore and Aft'

The evening blanket of darkness was benign and gentle. The stars were out, the wind still and the air soft and silky. The South Atlantic moon was in retreat. All was quiet at the Consulate. Girls giggled and shrieked in the distance. Someone was playing the Beatles. Reggae competed from Ladder Hill.

I went down the steps of Wellington House, past The Castle, through the arch and along beside the sea wall, past the Customs office, the cargo sheds, the containers and the cranes to the landing. The sea was smooth, unruffled, swells slumbering - as if it were never otherwise. The lights of sixty small craft twinkled in James Bay. And on a stagnating rusted drug ship. The *RMS* was due back from Ascension at midnight. Tomorrow by day, it would be different. The giant of the waterfront would be aroused and active.

When I returned, two old women were sitting on their front steps a door or two away from where I was staying.

"Good evening ladies," I said. It seemed unkind to breach their silent reverie.

"Good evening, sir."

"And it really is a good evening. One on which we can be thankful to be alive and to be so blessed as to know it."

"Yes" one said "you right sir, praise the Lord. It a noice quoiet place, St. Helena. You can sleep outside, sir, an' no-one will harm you. Unless you drunk an' the police bring you in. Yes. Lie on dat bench over dere all night an' you' money in you' pocket nex' mornin'. Safe an' soun'. Jus' like Jesus lookin' after you hisself. You t'ink he hear o' St. Helena, sir?"

"Yes. I am sure."

"Tat good t'en. We sleep peaceful."

Colonial Reports: 1928

HISTORY

St. Helena

There is an abundance of interesting historical and descriptive records concerning St. Helena. The archives of the Administration from 1678 are preserved at the Castle; among them is the original of the instrument 'The Laws and Constitution of the Island of St. Helena' issued by Charles II in 1681.

The island was discovered on 21st May, 1502, St. Helena's day, by Juan da Nova Castella, Commodore of a Portuguese squadron returning from India. The Portuguese made no attempt to make a colony of the island but were content to maintain it as a place of 'refreshment' for their ships by planting fruit trees and vegetables and introducing goats, pigs and wildfowl, including pheasants and partridges. It was the practice of the Portuguese to land on the island sick persons of a ship's company, 'whom they suspect will not live till they get home; these they leave to refresh themselves, and take away the year following, with the other fleet, if they live so long.'

The discovery of the island is said to have been kept a secret until the Englishman, Captain Cavendish, returning from a voyage round the world, anchored there on 8th June, 1588. He found on the island a great abundance of fruit and vegetables, thousands of goats, a great store of swine and wild fowl (the pheasants 'big and fat surpassing those which are in our country in bigness and numbers in a company'). He found also 'divers handsome buildings and houses, one, particularly, was a church tiled, and whitened on the outside very fair.' The only human inhabitants were three slaves and from them Captain Cavendish learnt the news that 'the East Indian fleet all laden with spices and Callicut cloth, with store of treasure, and very rich stones and pearls, were gone but twenty days before we came hither.'

St. Helena now became a place for 'the English, Portugals, Spaniards, and Hollanders to refresh themselves in going, but, for the most part, in returning from the Indies, it being sufficient to furnish ships with provisions for their voyage, here being salt to preserve the meat from stinking; and besides the air is so healthful that they often left their sick people there, who, in a short time, are restored to perfect health.' 'The greatest convenience of this island for ships' reported an English seaman 'is the plenty and goodness of the water.'

Eventually in 1645 the Dutch assumed possession of the island, but a few years later abandoned it to establish themselves at the Cape of Good Hope. Their place in St. Helena was taken by the English and in 1661 the Crown granted to the East India Company a charter for its administration.

According to some accounts the island was recaptured in 1665 by the Dutch, who were expelled the same year. They seized it again in 1672. The English Governor and his followers made their escape in English and French ships to Brazil. There they met an English squadron under the command of Captain (afterwards Sir Richard) Munden, who determined to recover possession of the island. He arrived off St. Helena on the evening of 14th May, 1673, and was fortunate in finding that no look-out was being kept. He landed a shore party at Prosperous Bay, as it came to be called in commemoration of the exploit. There the most active man of the party climbed up a precipice, taking with him a ball of twine to which was attached a rope by means of which the rest of the party were hauled up. The cliff thereafter became known as 'Holdfast Tom,' the urgent admonition of his comrades to the intrepid climber. As the ships appeared off Jamestown the landing party reached the heights above the town and the Dutch surrendered without striking a blow.

St. Helena reverted by conquest to the possession of the Crown. In December of 1673 a new charter was granted to the East India Company and, with the exception of the term of Napoleon's exile, the island continued under the Company's administration until 22nd

April, 1834, when it was brought under the direct control of the Crown.

The Colony is now administered by a Governor aided by an Executive Council. The Governor alone makes ordinances, there being no legislative council, but power is reserved to legislate by Order of His Majesty in Council.

The East India Company, in the terms of their Charter of 1673, attached importance to the island as 'very necessary and commodious for refreshing their servants and people in theire retournes homewards, being often then weak and decayed in their health by reason of their long voyages under their hott clymes.' This service the island continued to render during the period of the Company's administration. It had no possibilities as a trading station, and it remained purely a rendezvous for the protection and refreshment of shipping. The Governorship was often a reward for good service in India, and other offices were filled from time to time by the Company's servants whose health had suffered in the East.

With the disappearance of the Company's administration went its lavish expenditure and its high scale of salaries. The economy of Crown administration and consideration for the British taxpayer ushered in more difficult and less prosperous times for the inhabitants. The substitution of steam for sail and the opening of the Suez Canal meant the ruin of St. Helena as a shipping port. A century ago the number of ships calling each year was five hundred; today the number is forty, and in this era of cold storage supplies are rarely needed. More recently the removal of the garrison, in 1906-07, appeared at the time a crushing blow to the island. But the departure of the troops was not an unmixed evil, for it threw the island for the first time on its own resources and led to the creation of the fibre industry on which today the welfare of the inhabitants has come greatly to depend. The future of St. Helena lies in its agriculture and in the character and technical training of its people; it is probable, also, that before long the scenery and the climatic advantages of the island may gain it a reputation as a resort for those who favour quietude and simple living.

St. Helena has become famous in history as the scene of the Emperor Napoleon's exile and death. The house occupied by him at Longwood and the site of the tomb in Sane Valley where his remains lay for twenty years till their removal in 1840 are now in the charge of the French Government, who were granted the freehold in 1858.

From its earliest days, St. Helena appears to have been regarded as a place eminently suitable for exile or for the confinement of political prisoners.

The first exile to land on the island was Fernando Lopez in 1513. He was a Portuguese nobleman who had deserted his countrymen in India and turned apostate. Following on a Portuguese success near Goa he was surrendered to Albuquerque on condition that his life should be spared. His nose, his ears, his right hand, and the little finger of his left hand were cut off and he was thus placed on ship for Portugal. Rather than arrive in his country mutilated and disgraced he was at his own request left on shore at St. Helena with a few slaves. He remained on the island for four years, when on instructions from home he was removed to Portugal.

During the administration of the East India Company, St. Helena was selected for the confinement of an offending rajah who, however, did not survive the voyage. On two occasions Zulu rebels, amongst their number Dinuzulu, Cetewayo's son, have been received on the island as political prisoners. During the South African War full advantage was taken of St. Helena's natural advantages as a place of internment. About 4,500 prisoners of war, among them General Kronje, were sent to the island. Their presence brought a wave of prosperity to the island, but apart from that happy circumstance the Boers soon gained and have retained the good will and respect of the inhabitants.

St. Helena had intimate associations with the suppression of the slave trade between West Africa and the Americas.

Slave ships captured by British warships were brought to the island of condemnation, and a settlement for freed slaves was founded at Rupert's Bay. A few found employment locally, but about 10,000 were conveyed to the West Indies and British Guiana.

From time to time St. Helena has had the good fortune to attract interesting and eminent visitors. In 1676 Halley, the astronomer, then a student at Oxford, arrived in the island to determine the positions of the fixed stars of the Southern Hemisphere, and left his name behind him in 'Halley's Mount.' His observations were to some extent, it is said, hampered by mist and cloud. The same fate about one hundred years later, in 1761, awaited the observations of Dr. Maskelyne and Mr. Waddington, who visited the island to watch the transit of Venus on 6th June.

Captain Cook landed in the island in 1771 and again in 1774. He wrote that 'the children and descendants of the English in St. Helena are remarkable for their ruddy complexion and robust constitution.' 'As for the genius and temper of these people,' he observed, 'they seemed to be the most hospitable ever met with of English extraction, having scarce any tincture of avarice and ambition.'

Darwin arrived in St. Helena on 8th July, 1836. St. Helena, he was of opinion, had existed as an island from a very remote epoch. He remarked on 'the English, or rather Welsh, character of the scenery': 'When we consider that the number of plants now found on the island is 746, and out of these 52 alone are indigenous species, the rest having been imported, we see the reason of the British character of the vegetation.'

In August, 1910, HRH the Duke of Connaught called at the island, while on his way to open the first Parliament of the Union of South Africa, and in August, 1925, HRH the Prince of Wales spent two days at St. Helena on his way from South Africa to South America.

There still remains on the island one survivor of the Napoleonic period, the giant tortoise at Plantation, said by some authorities to be the oldest known living inhabitant of the world. One report states that this tortoise and a companion who died in 1918 were brought to St. Helena during the Governorship of General Beatson, 1808-13, and that they originally belonged to the French Artillery at Port Louis, being handed over to the British with the ordnance and stores at the capitulation of Mauritius in 1810. Melliss, writing in 1875, mentions a report that the tortoises had lived at Plantation for a century or more.

When he wrote they appeared to be fully grown, easily carrying a man.

GOVERNORS OF ST. HELENA

UNDER THE EAST INDIA COMPANY		UNDER THE CROWN	
Captain John Dutton	1659	Maj-Gen. George Middlemore	1836
Captain Robert Stringer	1661	Colonel Hamelin Trelawny	1842
Captain Richard Coney	1671	Maj-Gen. Sir Patrick Ross	1846
Captain Anthony Beale	1672	Col. Sir Thomas Gore Brown	1851
Sir Richard Munden	1673	Sir E. Hay Drummond Hay	1856
Captain Richard Kegwin	1673	Admiral Sir Charles Elliot	1863
Captain Gregory Field	1674	Vice Admiral C.G.E. Patey	1870
Major John Blackmore	1678	Hudson Ralph Janisch	1873
Captain Joshua Johnson	1690	W. Grey Wilson	1890
Captain Richard Kelinge	1693	Robert Armitage Sterndale	1897
Captain Stephen Poirier	1697	Lt-Col. Sir Henry Galway	1903
Captain John Roberts	1708	Major Sir Harry Cordeaux	1912
Captain Benjamin Boucher	1711	Colonel Robert Peel	1920
Captain Isaac Pyke	1714	Sir Charles Harper	1925
Edward Johnson	1719	Sir Spencer Davis	1932
Captain John Smith	1723	Sir Guy Pilling	1938
Edward Byfeld	1727	Major William Bain Gray	1941
Captain Isaac Pyke	1731	Sir George Joy	1947
John Goodwin	1738	Sir James Harford	1954
Captain Robert Jenkins	1741	Robert Alford	1958
Major Thomas Lambert	1742	Sir John Field	1962
Colonel David Dunbar	1744	Sir Dermod Murphy	1968
Charles Hutchinson	1747	Thomas Oates	1971
John Skottowe	1764	Geoffrey Guy	1977
Daniel Corneille	1782	John Dudley Massingham	1981
Colonel Robert Brooke	1787	Francis Eustice Baker	1984
Colonel Robert Patton	1802	Robert Frederick Stimson	1988
Maj-Gen. Alexander Beatson	1808	Alan Norman Hoole	1991
Colonel Mark Wilks	1813		
Lt-Gen. Sir Hudson Lowe	1816		
Brig-Gen. Alexander Walker	1823		
Brig-Gen Charles Dallas	1828		

WHITEWOOD

CABBAGE TREE

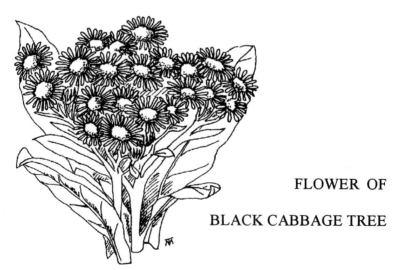

FLOWER OF

BLACK CABBAGE TREE

EXTRACT FROM A LETTER WRITTEN ON BOARD
THE *ASTROLABE* 9TH SEPTEMBER 1840
AND PUBLISHED IN *THE TIMES* OF LONDON
ON 2ND DECEMBER THAT YEAR

We cast anchor at St. Helena on the 7th of this month. The entire island was in a state of great excitement; for the expected arrival of the French ships of war which are destined to remove from amongst them the remains of their Illustrious captive make them imagine that all the sails which appear in the horizon belong to the expected convoy. Two days only were allowed us at St. Helena; and you will readily imagine that I profited by this interval to visit a tomb which will so soon lose its absorbing interest. It is but a league from Jamestown, the place of anchorage, to the tomb; but the road, though as well kept as possible, is a difficult one, winding itself zigzag along the rocky slides of precipitous hills . .

We walked over green turf, little disturbed, and preserving all its freshness. We leant over an iron railing remarkable for its simplicity, and then my eyes fell on a large stone level with the ground on which no letters were traced. The slab is void and naked; it has so much to say that it remains silent; and it does well. The enclosure is studded with a few sombre yewtrees, and above the tomb some willows droop their branches. Within the iron railing, and close to the flagstone which covers the Emperor's remains, are to be seen a tuft of lilies, and a stalk of geranium, planted by the hand of Madame Bertrand, a lingering witness of friendship and devotion . .

I should add that the French expedition is daily expected. A vessel of war has been sent from England to assist at the ceremony. All the necessary preparations for giving up the corpse of Napoleon to the French Prince are concluded. Near the tomb we obtained a sight of the apparatus with which the body is to be lifted. It is hoped that the corpse may be raised without removing the immense granite stone which covers the tomb, the English being anxious to preserve it in its present form, in the hope that the deserted sepulchre may still attract, if not the same number of pilgrims, at least some curious persons.

The remains of Napoleon are enclosed in four coffins. The first is tin, the next mahogany, the third is lead, and the whole is enclosed in a fourth coffin of mahogany. The grave is 12 feet in depth. The bottom is wrought in stone masonry, and the sarcophagus was placed on four piles, with a view to preseerve it from the damp. Above it is placed a large stone, then mason work 4 feet in thickness, earth above this, and over the whole lies a large flagstone.

PRESENT ASPECT OF ST. HELENA.

The following is an extract from a letter written on board the Astrolabe, the 9th of September :—

"We cast anchor at St. Helena on the 7th of this month. The entire island was in a state of great excitement; for the expected arrival of the French ships of war which are destined to remove from amongst them the remains of their illustrious captive make them imagine that all the sails which appear in the horizon belong to the expected convoy. Two days only were allowed us at St. Helena; and you will readily imagine that I profited by this interval to visit a tomb which will so soon lose its absorbing interest. It is but a league from James-town, the place of anchorage, to the tomb; but the road, though as well kept as possible, is a difficult one, winding itself zigzag along the rocky sides of precipitous hills. From the crest of one of these hills you look down into a deep and narrow valley, formerly called 'the Devil's Punchbowl,' and to-day 'the Valley of the Tomb.' We descended, and the man who accompanied us said, 'Here it is.' I was somewhat disappointed, having figured to myself some exterior solemnity, a sentinel at the least. Meanwhile the keeper took his keys, and, opening a frail wooden door, we found ourselves in the narrow enclosure, which is now the whole property of him to whom the whole continent of Europe once belonged.

"We walked over green turf, little disturbed, and preserving all its freshness. We leant over an iron railing remarkable for its simplicity, and then my eyes fell on a large stone level with the ground, on which no letters were traced. The slab is void and naked; it has so much to say that it remains silent; and it does well. The enclosure is studded with a few sombre yewtrees, and above the tomb some willows droop their branches. Within the iron railing, and close to the flagstone which covers the Emperor's remains, are to be seen a tuft of lilies, and a stalk of geranium, planted by the hand of Madame Bertrand, a lingering witness of friendship and devotion. The keeper was good enough to permit me to gather one of these leaves.

"Before leaving the enclosure we drank some water from the fountain, to which Napoleon came almost every day to refresh himself. We descended to the distance of about 200 paces to refresh ourselves at the house of Mrs. Cobbett, where it was the ex-Emperor's habit to go frequently, for the purpose of resting himself and conversing. This female showed us some souvenirs of Napoleon, and praised his kindness of disposition. Thence we went to Longwood, the exile's abode, which is now converted into a mill, and which no one can enter without paying in advance the sum of 3s. to the owner. On traversing the apartments, which were mean even in the days of their splendour, our conductor said to us—"Here was Napoleon's bed," and in its place you see a pair of horses standing—it is now a stable!

"The heights are all commanded by forts. The whole coast, too, bristles with them, and as many cannon may be counted as there are men in the garrison, the number being 400. During Napoleon's captivity the number of soldiers stationed in the island was 4,000. To-day the entire population of the island, consisting of the garrison, European residents, slaves, and a few Chinese, does not exceed this figure; and most certainly, once the remains of Napoleon leave it, it will be found to decrease. The commercial prosperity of St. Helena will feel the change as much, perhaps still more, since at the present day there is not a vessel coming from the Cape with passengers which is not obliged by a previous agreement to touch at James-town. The commerce of the island with China is now at an end, and every thing is excessively dear.

"I should add, that the French expedition is daily expected. A vessel of war has been sent from England to assist at the ceremony. All the necessary preparations for giving up the corpse of Napoleon to the French Prince are concluded. Near the tomb we obtained a sight of the apparatus with which the body is to be lifted. It is hoped that the corpse may be raised, without removing the immense granite stone which covers the tomb, the English being anxious to preserve it in its present form, in the hope that the deserted sepulchre may still attract, if not the same number of pilgrims, at least some curious persons.

"The remains of Napoleon are enclosed in four coffins. The first is tin, the next mahogany, the third is lead, and the whole is enclosed in a fourth coffin of mahogany. The grave is 12 feet in depth. The bottom is wrought in stone masonry, and the sarcophagus was placed on four piles, with a view to preserve it from the damp. Above it is placed a large stone, then mason work 4 feet in thickness, earth above this, and over the whole lies a large flagstone. In the fear that the exterior coffin may have been injured, a new one has been made to replace it.

"I have seen the funereal car which is destined to transport the corpse from the tomb to James-town. It is long, of a quadrangular form, supported by four wheels, and covered by a dome resting on four pillars, and surmounted by a funereal pall. The entire is covered with black cloth, fringed with crape. It will be drawn by four horses, entirely covered with black crape. I had the good fortune to find myself, at the period of examining this car, side by side with the two engineers, one of whom is charged to-day with the duty of extracting the corpse from the tomb, and the other was intrusted in 1821 with the superintendence of the ex-Emperor's obsequies. To these gentlemen I am indebted for the details recorded in this letter."

Facsimile letter, in full, from *The Times* from which the extract is given above.

His Royal Highness Prince Andrew, Duke of York, has honoured the book with a Foreword. It was done after his visit to the *RMS St. Helena* at Cardiff Docks on 22nd December 1992.

* * *

Writing of this kind is made possible by a variety of people who contribute to the development of its concepts and content in many ways. The author becomes a listener, a catalyst, an interpreter and hopefully an acceptable scribe.

I am especially grateful for the sustained encouragement and support of His Excellency Alan N. Hoole, OBE, Governor and Commander-in-Chief of St. Helena, and his wife Delia; similarly to Andrew Bell, his fellow directors and staff of Curnow Shipping Limited at Porthleven; to Tom Chellew for Cable & Wireless plc., and to my publisher and editor Diana Holderness of Wilton 65 for proposing and achieving a greatly enhanced illustrated finished product.

There were many Saints and Tristanians - men and women, young and old - whose participatory, if at times involuntary, help I must recognise. They appear in the text, named and unnamed. My special thanks are due to Ray and Ivy Ellick in London; Cynthia and Dougie Bennett, who transcribed my early writing and shared their 'flu-stricken reactions with me; Rodney Buckley, David Clarke, John Cranfield, Basil George, Tony Leo and Joy Laurence of Radio St. Helena, Julie and Malvin Laurence, Cecil Charles Maggott, Desmond Wade and Joan Yon.

On Voyage 6 South and North of the *RMS St. Helena*, the Master, officers and crew, Saints and British alike, together with my fellow passengers, helped to make my time at sea varied, pleasurable and tolerably productive - once we disposed of an assumption by some that, because of my frequent withdrawal symptoms and cabin work schedule, I was a commercial espionage implant in their midst. Jim Kerr, lately Education Officer on Tristan Da Cunha, found time to read through the Tristan chapters as Voyage 6 drew to a close in Cardiff.

In Britain, former Second Purser Angie Reid laboured into the night on her newly-acquired word processor for many weeks and weekends. Clive Warren at ODA cast a constructively critical eye over the first draft. He contributed equally helpfully to the factual sections on the *RMS* and in other respects. It was comforting to have the script passed ODA-fit for public consumption! A first draft appraisal and detailed latter-day text checks and proof-reading by Sanford K. Smith were invaluable preparation for my own. All this notwithstanding, responsibility for the final text is, of course, entirely mine.

My thanks go to Michael Howorth for his energetic imaginativeness; to his wife Frances, for her splendid colour plates, which together with the other illustrations, bring visual life to the text; to all those mentioned by Diana Holderness in her Editor's Note; and to Elizabeth Purves and the staff of the reference section of the Kent County Council library services at Sevenoaks.

Any omission on my part is unintentional; and may be explained - even excused - by a singular irony. I prepare this from a horizontal position on the floor of my bedroom. My back caved in as a result of the inexplicably sudden onset of acute pain spasms a few days ago; an irony because it was this affliction which put me similarly out of action in the Judges Lodge at Seaview on St. Helena during my second ODA Budgetary Aid Review mission in 1986.

Could it be that the Saints have 'put their finger 'pon me' a second time?

Kenneth Bain

Sevenoaks
Kent

15th August 1993

Note: The story of Niuafo'ou (Tin Can Island) first appeared in my THE FRIENDLY ISLANDERS, 1967

We were glad, together with Frances and Michael Howorth, to be asked to publish Kenneth Bain's new book on St. Helena. Bigger publishing houses did not feel able to commit themselves to the many illustrations which the author felt essential. All the colour photographs were taken by Frances Howorth.

With the support of the Overseas Development Administration, Curnow Shipping and Cable & Wireless, we have enjoyed preparing the book for publication. The author allowed us to keep our house style for page numbering combined with headers, and similarly we have agreed to accept his usage for inverted commas, multiple full stops at the beginning and end of paragraphs, and more italics than we would choose. I hope that this amicable mixture of give and take has resulted in a book which is pleasant to read and to handle.

Everyone whom we have approached for help and advice has generously given it. Among others, Alan Hoole – Governor from 1991, Dorothy Evans, Nick Thorpe, Trevor Hearl, Rosemary Laurent, and Emily O'Bey have lent, tracked down, or told us how to find necessary photographs. The Wirebird and Count Bertrand's house were drawn by June Tyler. Thanks are also due to Shirley Sargent for much work in our office, and to her husband who copied the Tristan albatross. A thank you also to Andrew Kirk in the F. C. O. for his helpful research in relation to Tristan da Cunha.

We are grateful for invaluable support from the House of Lords Library, among other things for obtaining the Times extract for reproduction in Appendix III, and borrowing Melliss' *St. Helena,* from the London Library. This enabled us to select many suitable indigenous plants for inclusion in watermark style from Tracey Mitchell's line drawings (to distinguish them from pictures directly related to the text). In listing the plants we have attempted to follow the most recently accepted sources. Tracey did many other drawings including the Breadfruit tree from pictures made available by the Royal Botanical Gardens at Kew.

Mark Buttle gave to Fiona Rowland skilled technical advice and help. Together they tackled the major part of the typesetting. My husband, Richard, compiled the Index and has tried to include all people and places relevantly mentioned in the book; but omitting those to whom the text makes only incidental reference. As is usual, the Appendices have not been indexed.

Explanation is needed for the shadow tricoleur flag shown with The Briars Pavilion and Count Bertrand's house (see Appendix III). It was impracticable to show it in the coloured illustration of Longwood where it properly belongs. There is no South African flag shown, as this is not generally flown at the Boer Cemetery. Two basic sketch maps are included early in the book – one to show the position of the islands in the South Atlantic, and the other of St. Helena showing as many as possible of the places mentioned. Allan Crawford allowed us to reproduce his detailed plan of Tristan da Cunha as well as the albatross, and Simon Winchester to quote from his *Outposts.* This quotation has been reproduced by permission of the publishers, Hodder & Stoughton.

From anyone not mentioned we would ask forgiveness. We have been enormously encouraged by the kindness of all whom we have approached for advice and assistance.

Diana Holderness
1993

Ascension Island 8,30,68-9,81
Bahraini Exiles 99
Bain, Margaret (Mrs. Kenneth Bain) 176
Baker, F.E. (Governor 1984) 161-3,176
Bell, Andrew, founder of Curnow
Shipping 8,23,120,158,160,170,172,174
Bell, Prue (Mrs. Andrew Bell),23
Benjamin, Eric 62-3
Benjamin, Second Engineer Myron
    24-6,171
Bennett, Cynthia (Mrs. Dougie Bennett)
    30,39-40
Bennett, Dougie 30
Bishop of St. Helena 175
Bligh, Captain William RN 84-9
Blue Hill 104
Boer War 80; Prisoners 97-8;
    Deadwood Plain and Broad Bottom
    Camps 97; Peace Camp 97;
    repatriation 97; Knollcombes
    cemetery 97-8
Breadfruit 84,86,89-90
Briars, The 6,39,60,66,79,82,84,163
Brig *Afoisant* 85
Brooke, Lt. Col Robert (Governor 1792)
    85,88
Buckley, Sylvia 68
Button Up Corner 79

Cable & Wireless 39,79-83
Cape of Good Hope 149
Cape Point 149
Castle, The 32,51,75,84,113,178
Castle archives 84
Cedar Vale 101-3
Chellew, Tom 81
Chevrolet Charabanc (Reg. No.82)
    40,79
Christian, Radio Officer Tom 129
Clarke, David 101
Cleugh's Plain 100
Clingham, Sgt. Smokey 48
Corker, Cecil,40,79
Corker, Colin 40

Crawford, Allan 132
Cronje, General 97
Croston, Third Engineer Wally 170
Crown Agents 173
Cudd, Chief Officer Cyril 'Spud' 113
CurnowShipping 8,24,36,103,119,121,
    128,154,156-171,172-7

Dallas, Brig.-Gen. (Governor 1834) 73
Dalmeida, Raphael 116
da Nova Castella, Juan, Admiral 8
Dellar, Chief Purser Colin 119, 127
de Rebello, Daphne 3
Devil's Punch Bowl 79
Diaz, Bartholomew, navigator 8
Dust, Victor Gonzalez 14-6, 23
Dutton, Captain John (Governor 1659)
    72-3

East India Company 85, 93, 99
Ellick, Ivy (Mrs. Ray Ellick) 3
Ellick, Ray 3

Francis, Cabin Steward Michael 114
Francis Plain 38, 41, 93
French Consul 6
French territory 6

George, Chief Education Officer Basil
    32-3
George, Joy 38
George, Tommy 9-10
Glass, Lewis, Chief Islander
    Tristan da Cunha 139
Glass, Mrs. Lewis 139
Glass, William 129
Guinness Book of Records 26, 41,
    126-7, 130

Hagan, Colin (Doc) 134
Half Tree Hollow (The City)
    67,93,105,149
Heart Shape Waterfall 79
Henry, Nigel 16-8, 19

Henry, Vilma 101-3
High Knoll Fort 79, 82
High Point 102
HMS Bounty 84
HMS Providence 85
Hone, Chief Officer Bob 113, 115-7,
    153, 155
Hoole, Alan (Governor 1991) 6,48,51-2,
    113,119,138-9,154,173-6
Hoole, Delia (Mrs. Alan Hoole)48-50,
    139,154,173,175
Hopkins, Cathy (Mrs. Keith Hopkins) 64-6
Hopkins, Keith 65
Houghton, Rev: Michael 168
HRH, Prince Andrew, Duke of York 34,
    77,167,176-7
Huxtable, Cadet Robert 27

James Bay 27,33,169,178
Jamestown 9; landing at the port 36;
    Grand Square 58;Courthouse 58,62;
    Legislative Council Chamber 58;
    Public Library 58; Jacob's Ladder 42;
    Ladder Hill 60,67,93,100,166,169,178;
    Consulate Hotel 91; Wellington House
    (Yon's Café) 178; Side Path 60,79
Johnson, Rt. Rev: James (former Bishop
    of St. Helena) 177
Joshua, Patrick 41

Knutsford, 1st Viscount 95

Lawrence, Julie (Mrs. Malvin Lawrence)
    100
Lawrence, Malvin 100
Laws of St. Helena for 1990 51
Longwood House 6,7,48,65,79

Maggott, Cecil 84-5,99
Makarios, Archbishop 99
Martin, Geoffrey William
    (Chief Justice, 1992) 61
Massingham, John (Governor 1981) 159
McDaniel, Belfred 105

McWhirter, Norris 26,126-8

NAAFI 68-69
Napoleon Bonaparte 7,19,74,128
Ndabuko 95-96
Nicholls, Alan 21
Niuafo'ou (Tin Can Island)
    1,142,147,148

Oman Sea One 82, 112-9
Overseas Development Administration
    (ODA) 14,24,28,37,123,158,160-1,
    163-5,170, 172-6

Pauncefort, Bernard 134,137
Piccolo Hill 33
Pitcairn Island 1,3,41,53,120,128
Plantation House 6,8,49,52,65,73,
    92-4,154
Pridham, Gordon 104
Pridham, Ruth (Mrs. Gordon Pridham)
    104
Prince Andrew School, 9,19,38,64-5,
    69,169

Read, Second Purser Angie 133
Repetto, Radio Officer Andy 129
Repetto, Darren 134
Repetto, Nurse, SRN 132
Ricketts, Sir Robert 7
Ricketts, Theresa (Lady) 7
RMS St. Helena Island, replaced in
November 1990 by the present ship,
RMS St. Helena, 9,14,19,22-6,31,
    33,34,36-7,41,43,53,65,69-70,
    77,79,83,93,103,107,109,
    112-9,121,122-3,126-8,
    133,135,139,149-155,159,
    167-171,175,177,178
Roberts, Captain David 173
Robson, Major Francis
    (Lieut. Governor 1792) 85,88
Rosemary Plain 102
Ruperts Bay 71
Ruperts Valley 80

St. Helena 4,6; discovery 8;
  financial support 9; Legislative
  Council 10,64; Legal Department 21;
  appearance of Saints 30; diabetes 31;
  1988 Constitution order 53;
  subsidy 53; table of precedence 54-5;
  lack of natural resources 70;
  canning company 70; cleanliness of
  island 74; Captain Bligh's visit 84-9;
Has-nots 107-8; Has 109-111;
  History 179-184; Governors 185
St. Helena Guardian 95
St. Helena News 31, 169
St. Helena News Review 48
St. Martin-in-the-Fields 12-3
St. Martin-in-the-Hills 13
St. Paul's Church 73
Sandy Bay 101, 104
Seaview 31,79
Shingana 96-7
Smith, Captain Martin 151-4, 167-170,
  173,175
Smith, Sanford 23
Spry, Sir John Farley
  (Chief Justice 1983) 58
Spry, Stella (Lady) 59
Sterndale, R.A. (Governor 1897) 96
Stevens, George 39,80-2
Stroud, Chef David 133
Stroud, Stedson 101-4
Sugrue, Simon 173
Swain, Sailor Julian 115,120-1,122,
  134-5,139

Tenerife 1,14,83
Thompson's Hill 102
Thorpe, Nick 22-3
Tonga, Kingdom of 1,142-8
Trafalgar Square 13
Tristan da Cunha 1,8,71,120-141,
  142
Tussauds 12-3
Two Gun Saddle 79

Union Castle Ships 150,156

Wallace, Douglas 70
Warren, Clive 14,44,158,162-6
White, Ron 174
Williams, Supt. Engineer Mark 170-1
Williams, Bosun Pat 115
Wilson, Radio Officer Bob 112,114,
  119,150
Wilson, W.G. (Governor 1890) 95
Wrangham, William 85,88
Wyatt, Captain Bob 113-4,115,117-8,
  153-5,168,173

Yon, Third Engineer David 115
Young, Second Mate Rodney
  (School Bus) 10,27,115,167,170

Zulus 95-7